D0568821

COLORADO

COLORADO

A History in Photographs

RICHARD N. ELLIS

AND

DUANE A. SMITH

UNIVERSITY PRESS OF COLORADO

10 9 8 7 6 5 4 3 2 1

The University Press of Colorado is a cooperative publishing enterprise supported, in part, by Adams State College, Colorado State University, Fort Lewis College, Mesa State College, Metropolitan State College of Denver, University of Colorado, University of Northern Colorado, University of Southern Colorado, and Western State College.

LIBRARY OF CONGRESS CATALOGING-IN-PUBLICATION DATA

Ellis, Richard N., 1939–
    Colorado: a history in photographs / Richard N. Ellis and Duane A. Smith.
      p. cm.
    Includes index.
    ISBN 0-87081-219-x (alk. paper).
    1. Colorado — History — Pictorial works. 2. Colorado — Description and travel — Views. I. Smith, Duane A. II. Title.
    F777.E45 1991
    978.8 — dc20   91-34157
                                                        CIP

For Luann and Gay

CONTENTS

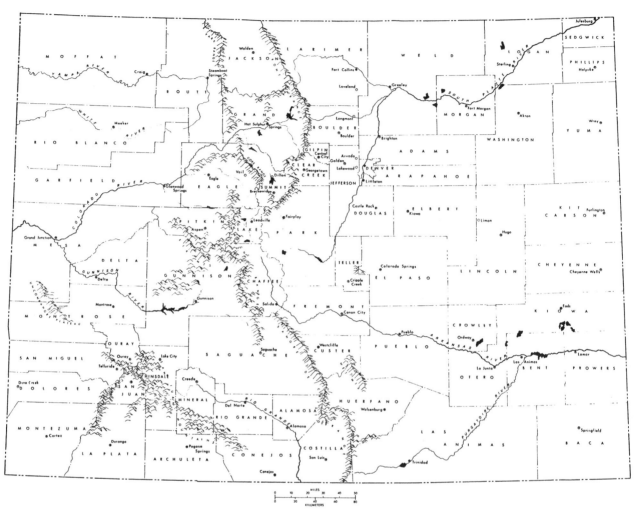

Reprinted from Kenneth A. Erickson and Albert W. Smith, *Atlas of Colorado* (Boulder: Colorado Associated University Press, 1985).

PROLOGUE

Colorado Day 1991 — one hundred fifteen years have passed since that exciting August 1, 1876, when Colorado became the Centennial State. As a writer from Oro City explained to the readers of the *Engineering and Mining Journal* in an August 20 letter, "We were so elated at the admission of our bright young Territory to the honors of Statehood, that between that event and the celebration of the Centennial Fourth, we had hardly room for a thought of work all July." Only eighteen years earlier, the gold that would lead to the legendary 1859 Pike's Peak gold rush had been discovered. That rush brought permanent settlement to the region.

Time seemed compressed to those pioneering Coloradans. Fast-moving developments in the years before statehood gave them the impression that the years were passing more swiftly than they actually were. Oro City had already experienced a placer mining boom and bust, moved its townsite nearer to the hard-rock mines, found itself in the backwash of territorial mining, and now stood on the threshold of an even greater bonanza. Mining camps had been born, died, and had faded into ghost towns. The Civil War had become history: the guns in the states and in this western territory had been silenced. At first, Colorado was hailed as a second California but more recently had found itself disparaged as a territory with little mining potential. The Cheyennes and Arapahoes no longer inhabited the eastern plains, and the Utes found themselves tenuously hanging onto their lands to the west. A generation of Coloradans had dreamed, worked, and watched their fortunes rise and fall with those of their adopted home.

These were invigorating years that, fortunately for future generations, have been preserved in records and photographs. It is with the latter, photographs, that this volume is preoccupied. Photography was new to Americans when the news of the Pike's Peak gold discoveries infiltrated the states. Even so, publisher

William Byers noted in his *Rocky Mountain News*, June 11, 1859, that already a "Mr. Welch" was "taking views with the apparatus in and around Denver and Auraria." The camera had come to Colorado with the fifty-niners and ever since has recorded the land, the people, and their lives.

Two years later, Byers was encouraging his readers to have a "true likeness taken of themselves, their stores, dwellings, mills or stock yards" to forward to friends back in the states. For the first time, the average American had the opportunity to seize immortality, or as Byers concluded, "secure the shadow, ere the substance perish." Many did just that in the decades that followed, and as a consequence they preserved their Colorado.

It was not as convenient or easy in those days to "secure the shadow" as it is today with high-speed film and cameras that incorporate the most advanced technology of the 1990s. William Henry Jackson, the most renowned and remembered of those early-day photographers, recalled:

> how onerous were the conditions imposed upon the old-time photographer. Then, the so-called "wet plate" was in general use, involving a complex process of many operations, and requiring practice and experience to attain the necessary manipulative skill. It was so messy chemically, and so encumbered with so much apparatus that there is little wonder that photography was rarely the hobby of amateurs and that the making of pictures by this means was almost wholly the work of professionals.

Photographs taken then, and later, captured a vanished Colorado, and they continue to open a window to provide a look back into yesterday.

So on Colorado Day 1991 it is appropriate to thank all the photographers, professional and amateur, who have perpetuated this aspect of Colorado's past. A deep debt of gratitude is also owed to those who preserved the photographs over the years. As the editor of Lake City's *Silver World* (July 8, 1876) shouted, "Three Cheers for the State of Colorado." Three more cheers and a generous thank you to the men and women who captured the "shadow" before it faded from memory.

RICHARD N. ELLIS
DUANE A. SMITH

ACKNOWLEDGMENTS

Colorado has a rich photographic history. This photographic legacy has been responsible for the production of many books, a number of which focus on major photographers such as William Henry Jackson, George Beam, or L. C. McClure. Some of these individuals, Jackson among them, are important not only in the history of photography in Colorado but also because they hold a significant place in the history of photography in America. Though one could easily compile a volume based largely on the work of these artistic giants, our main goal was to illustrate the history of Colorado without particular emphasis on the photographers themselves. In doing so, it was our desire to provide even coverage of geographical areas and of the major chronological periods in Colorado history. Thus, the subject matter of the photographs and their quality were of primary importance.

Before beginning this project, we were aware that there were important collections of photographs in institutions scattered across the state. Most notable and most used, of course, are the magnificent collections at both the Colorado Historical Society and the Western History Department of the Denver Public Library. These two collections cover a wide variety of subject areas and geographical regions. The photo archives of the Western Historical Collections at the University of Colorado also have a statewide focus. In contrast, the photo archives of institutions, such as the Museum of Western Colorado in Grand Junction, the Grand County Museum in Hot Sulphur Springs, the Pueblo Library District, the Pike's Peak Library District, and the Museum of Northwest Colorado in Craig, tend to concentrate on a more narrow geographical area. The collections of these and other institutions, however, are significant and should not be ignored by scholars. All of these institutions provided encouragement,

This project was made possible, in part, by a grant from the Colorado Endowment for the Humanities, and with the assistance of Fort Lewis College.

assistance, and support for this book. We wish to thank the following people and their staffs for helping to bring this project to fruition:

Adams State College
Alamosa, Colorado
Robert Kelly

Amon Carter
Fort Worth, Texas

The Aultman Museum of Photography
Trinidad, Colorado
Penny Bieber

Bud Werner Memorial Library and
   Tread of the Pioneers Museum
Steamboat Springs, Colorado
Chris Painter

Bureau of Reclamation
Denver, Colorado
Britt Storey

Ben Nighthorse Campbell
Ignacio, Colorado

Carnegie Branch Library
Boulder, Colorado
Lois Anderton

Carnegie Public Library
Trinidad, Colorado

City of Greeley Museums
Greeley, Colorado
Peggy Ford

Colorado College
Colorado Springs, Colorado
Judith Finley

Colorado Historical Society
Denver, Colorado

Colorado National Monument
Fruita, Colorado
Hank Schoch

Colorado Springs Pioneers Museum
Colorado Springs, Colorado
Sharron Uhler

Colorado State Archives
Denver, Colorado

Colorado State University
Fort Collins, Colorado
Dr. James E. Hansen, II

Walter Conrad
Bayfield, Colorado

Coors Brewing Company
Golden, Colorado
John Wood and John Meadows

Glenn Cuerden
Denver, Colorado

The Daily Camera
Boulder, Colorado
Laurence Paddock

Delta County Historical Society
Delta, Colorado
Esther Stephens

Denver Public Library/Western History
   Department
Denver, Colorado
Eleanor Gehres and Augie Mastrogiuseppe

Durango Herald
Durango, Colorado
Doug Storum

Durango/Purgatory Handicapped Sports
   Association
Beth Warren

Durango & Silverton Railroad
Durango, Colorado
Amos Cordova

Englewood Public Library
Englewood, Colorado
Nancy Bunker

Estes Park Area Historical Museum
Estes Park, Colorado
Mel Busch

M. K. Ferguson Co.
Albuquerque, New Mexico
Mark Thompson

Florence Pioneer Historical Museum
Florence, Colorado
Charles "Chopper" Price

Fort Collins Public Library
Fort Collins, Colorado
Karen McWilliams

Fort Lewis College/Center of Southwest
   Studies
Durango, Colorado
Catherine Conrad

Fort Morgan Museum
Fort Morgan, Colorado
Marne Jurgemeyer

Frontier Historical Society Museum
Glenwood Springs, Colorado
Janet Riley

Grand County Museum
Hot Sulphur Springs, Colorado
Betty Kilsdonk and Tracie Etheredge

Hiwan Homestead Museum
Evergreen, Colorado
Sandy Crain

Kansas Historical Society
Topeka, Kansas

La Plata County Historical Society
Durango, Colorado
Charles DiFerdinando and Robert
   McDaniel

Littleton Historical Museum
Littleton, Colorado
Linda Bushman

Loveland Museum and Gallery
Loveland, Colorado
Monica Gould and Tom Katsempalis

Mesa Verde National Park
Beverly Cunningham

The Mining Gallery
Leadville, Colorado

Montrose County Historical Society
   Museum
Montrose, Colorado
Marilyn Cox

Museum of Northwest Colorado
Craig, Colorado
Dan Davidson

Museum of Western Colorado
Grand Junction, Colorado
Judy Prosser-Armstrong

Tom Noel
Denver, Colorado

North Fork Historical Society/Paonia
   Public Library
Paonia, Colorado
Wallace Eubanks and Shirley Lund

Northern Colorado Water Conservancy
   District
Loveland, Colorado
Brian Werner

Ouray County Museum
Barbara L. Muntyan

Overland Trail Museum
Sterling, Colorado
Anna Mae Hagemeier

Laurence T. Paddock
Boulder, Colorado

Pike's Peak Library District
Colorado Springs, Colorado
Mary Davis

Pro Rodeo Hall of Fame
Colorado Springs, Colorado
Patricia Florence

Pueblo Library District
Pueblo, Colorado
Noreen Riffe and Joanne Dodds

Rifle Creek Museum
Rifle, Colorado
Kim Fazy

Rio Blanco Historical Society and White
   River Museum
Meeker, Colorado
Vern Rader

Rio Grande County Museum
Del Norte, Colorado
Mark Allison

Rocky Mountain Jewish Historical
  Society/University of Denver
Denver, Colorado
Dr. Jeanne Abrams

Jay Sanford
Arvada, Colorado

San Juan County Historical Society
Silverton, Colorado
Allen Nosaman

San Luis Museum
San Luis, Colorado
Juanita Gurule

Strater Hotel
Durango, Colorado
Rod Barker

United States Army Military History
  Research Collection
Carlisle Barracks, Pennsylvania

United States Geological Survey
  Photographic Library
Denver, Colorado
Joe McGregor

University of Colorado/Athletic
  Department/Media Relations
Boulder, Colorado
Dave Plati

University of Colorado/Western
  Historical Collections
Boulder, Colorado
Cassandra Volpe

Ute Pass Historical Society and Pikes Peak
  Museum
Woodland Park, Colorado
Jan Pettit

COLORADO

I

NOTHING IS IMPOSSIBLE
1859–1890

The hum of busy men is heard in the mountains so lately rising lonely in majestic silence; the cheerful tones of a multitude fill the air that has but lately echoed only the occasional voice of a weary wanderer ... Men are rapidly gathering together, towns are built, cities are in embryo formation, and all the paraphernalia of busy life are seen and heard 600 miles west of last year's outposts of civilization.

SO WROTE WILLIAM BYERS, the enthusiastic editor and proprietor of the *Rocky Mountain News*, in the inaugural edition of the paper (April 23, 1859). Byers started off sprinting, having set his mind to promoting, building, and saluting his new home. He never stopped to look back. An eager and optimistic 1859er, Byers concluded his first editorial in these words: "If the richness and extent of the Gold Regions realize their present promise, a new State will be organized west of Kansas and Nebraska ere this year is closed, with a hundred thousand inhabitants."

They became legends in their own time, those fifty-niners; they came west with high hopes, victims of a virulent case of gold fever. Some never recovered from that fever, or the subsequent silver virus. The whole world seemed to be at their beck and call. Neither they nor the land they poked, sluiced, and dug would ever be the same again. Not since 1849, with the stampede to California, had Americans seen anything like this. (Coincidentally, at the very same time, Californians were repeating their previous experience, this time stampeding east across the Sierra Nevadas to the silver-ribbed Comstock lode. In most of the country, however, news of the Pike's Peak rush completely overshadowed what came out of the far reaches of future Nevada.)

Out of this 1859 rush Colorado would eventually be born, the child of that American dream of getting rich without working. In the years that followed, a generation of Coloradans would continue to scramble for the elusive bonanza hidden somewhere in the mountain depths. Expecting to acquire wealth without effort, most found that they had never worked so hard before just to make a living. Only a very few became wealthy — just enough to encourage the rest to keep on rushing to the next mountain valley and up the nameless canyons into the depths of the Rocky Mountains.

They came west for reasons similar to those that drew Englishmen to Jamestown, Virginia, in 1607 and lured colonists into the dark and bloody bowels of Kentucky in the 1760s: opportunities for instant wealth, a fresh start, an escape from a drab life, and sheer adventure. The economic doldrums that enveloped the country after the harrowing crash of 1857, the darkening war clouds between North and South, and the sometimes unhealthful, fever-ridden climate of the Midwest pushed more than a few into action. However, the stories that this was a new, richer California — a "poor man's diggings" wealthy beyond imagination — motivated most of the movement toward the Pike's Peak country.

Stories of gold and silver in the central Rockies dated from the days of the Spanish. As the years went by, others, including Zebulon Pike, fur trappers, and travelers who ventured into high mountains, added more beguiling tidbits. By 1858, after forty-niners had contributed their accounts, the way had been paved for an invasion. That spring two groups, one from Kansas and another from Indian Territory (Oklahoma) and each unknown to the other, rode west to seek their fortunes.

The Russell party, headed by brothers Oliver, Green, and Levi, based its decision to start on the knowledge that gold had been found in June 1850 by some Cherokees on the way to California. The Lawrence, Kansas, party came because a Delaware army scout, Fall Leaf, had brought back gold from the 1857 Plains campaign. The fact that he refused to accompany their party, despite repeated inducements, should have served as a warning, but nothing could dampen the enthusiasm of these eager gold-seekers. By a somewhat circuitous route, these Cherokee and Delaware Indians eventually doomed their own contemporaries — the Utes, Cheyennes, and Arapahoes who called this land home — by drawing the white population westward.

After weeks of discouragement, most of the Russell party returned home. A determined remnant eventually found a small pocket of gold where Denver now sprawls. The Lawrence party spent time in the Pike's Peak region, and one of its members, Julia Holmes, became the first white woman to reach that mountain's top. The group had not come to Colorado just to see the sights, however, so it retreated to Fort Garland in the San Luis Valley to resupply and consider its options. Here it was that a mysterious mountain telegram brought rumors of the Russell party's discovery. At once, the Lawrence party raced north and joined the Russells. Not much gold was to be found during that late summer, so they all turned instead to that familiar frontier expedient, town planning. During this time, news of the discovery was being carried eastward in the hands of a trader, one John Cantrell, who had also visited the Russells. His announcement captured the attention of the press, created mounting excitement, and drove Americans to make plans for the trip west.

About 100,000 ventured forth, starting early in the spring. The first arrivals found the towns of Denver and Auraria awaiting them with inflated prices, but not much gold. Many turned back, denouncing the whole scene as a hoax; in some ways they were right. Much had been assumed, more had been dreamed, and too few realities had been understood. Fortunately for the future of Colorado, experienced miners George Jackson and John Gregory and a group of prospectors from Boulder, the would-be rival of Denver, ventured into the mountains. They found enough gold upon which to base a rush but remained secretive about their discoveries at future Idaho Springs, Central City, and Gold Hill.

By the time William Byers launched his *Rocky Mountain News*, word of these discoveries had spread, and the determined gold-seekers passed quickly through the little villages at the foothills in their haste to reach the mountains. There they unpacked their pans, picks, and shovels and set to placering for free gold. When the pan proved too slow and tiring, they followed the example of the forty-niners and advanced to the rocker method and then to the sluice box in order to work more gold-bearing gravel in a day. The north and south branches of Clear Creek (no longer running clear after the miners began dumping their placer tailings into the stream) were soon crowded with avid fifty-niners. Other prospectors moved farther on into South Park and by fall had crossed the Snowy Range into the Blue River drainage. They organized mining districts, created mining laws, and established the rudiments of government to give themselves some semblance of a legal basis for being there (they were, after all, trespassing on Indian land), but they generally believed that the least government was the best government.

These fifty-niners found the placer deposits less extensive than they had envisioned. Soon they were digging into the ground to follow mineral-bearing veins. This method required more money and experience as well as mills to crush and separate the gold, all of which were largely lacking in Pike's Peak country. When needed equipment and capital came, it arrived from the Midwest and the East, forming a tie that would bind for the next generation. California money and miners, tied up in the Comstock excitement, did not have the time for, or the interest in, prospects farther east.

Most of the fifty-niners had no mining experience and found their new occupation difficult, tiresome, and usually unprofitable. Many reverted to their previous occupations — some to farming in the river-watered valleys beyond the foothills, others to merchandising in the camps scattered near the mines. This was an urban frontier; towns sprang up overnight to provide services and supplies to the miners, who had little time for routine tasks but plenty of gold with which to pay blacksmiths, freighters, surveyors, clothiers, carpenters, and saloon keepers.

When fall turned to winter, large numbers of fifty-niners returned east or settled in Denver to escape the mountain snows. There they waited until the spring of 1860, when a second gold rush took place. However, with the nation nearing a crucial presidential election and becoming embroiled in a sectional crisis, the 1860 rush generated less interest than the previous year's. The new mining season drew prospectors into the Gunnison country and the far-distant and isolated San Juan Mountains. The biggest news, however, came from California Gulch, next to where Leadville would one day be, with the discovery of one more set of placer diggings. Hard-rock, or underground, mining was proving itself more durable, although the problems of the previous year — finances, isolation, and lack of experience — continued to thwart the miners who burrowed into the mountains.

Urbanization went on apace, with Denver emerging as the dominant community. Its favorable location, aggressive leadership, and possession of the lone permanent newspaper gave it advantages no other town could match. Although Byers and his *News* promoted and defended the entire Pike's Peak country, Denver's interests always came first and foremost. Byers's attitude was clearly stated in a March 10, 1861, editorial. Denver, he said, was destined to become the "metropolis of the Rocky Mountain region" and would be the "largest inland city on the American continent."

Aspiring politicians also came west with the miners to tap the golden opportunities that would become available with the creation of a new territory and, eventually, a new state. Unfortunately for them, the onrushing North-South controversy doomed all attempts to generate immediate federal action. Consequently, local organizers directed their efforts toward forming their own territory, calling it Jefferson. This step was supported by all those who wanted the assurance of a legal basis for owning land. Some action of this kind was necessary, because at that moment the region was divided among Kansas, Nebraska, Utah, and New Mexico territories, with Indian treaties further complicating the situation. During the winter of 1860–61, these pioneers dabbled in politics, holding an election and organizing a legislature. When the time came to pay, though, support melted away. Nobody favored taxing himself to play at government.

The coveted territorial status came during the secession crisis that same winter. When the Southern states marched out, the remaining Northern congressmen were more than willing to organize the free territory of Colorado. It remained for new president Abraham Lincoln and the Republicans to make the first territorial appointments, a job they embraced with enthusiasm. Washington would be controlled throughout the territorial years by the Republican party, a circumstance clearly reflected in Colorado politics. Until the turmoil of the 1890s, if one hoped to achieve success, he would have to follow the path that led through the Republican party.

The watershed Civil War years ended the first period of Colorado history and ushered in many of the themes that would dominate for the next generation. For example, Colorado's ties to the states back east and to the government in Washington would become more binding. The war strained this relationship and brought it more sharply into focus. Colorado would never be as "ruggedly independent" as some of its boosters so proudly claimed.

The war had other, more direct effects on Colorado. No battles were fought in the territory, but its troops played a major role in repelling the one serious threat of Confederate invasion at the battles of Glorieta Pass and Apache Canyon, New Mexico, in March 1862. Throughout the war years Colorado's governors, the excitable William Gilpin (1861–62) and the scholarly John Evans (1862–65), found themselves unable to secure much help from the Lincoln administration in meeting what they perceived as the territory's pressing needs. Washington was preoccupied with too many other problems to be concerned about those in the far-distant central Rockies.

A lack of money continued to plague the region. Indeed, the need to raise, equip and pay the troops of the First Colorado Regiment forced Gilpin to issue notes on the federal treasury, an action for which he had no authorization. When the treasury refused payment, the territorial economy shuddered, an outcry arose, and Gilpin hied himself to Washington to argue his case. He had become so controversial that Lincoln removed him and appointed Evans. The troops Gilpin raised proved their worth, but too late to save the governor.

Evans had more success in handling Southerners, most of whom had long since departed the territory anyway, but he ran into trouble with the Plains Indians. The governor was both a representative of the people and an Indian agent, an unworkable proposition. The two cultures had been clashing for centuries; Colorado simply reflected a continuation of the misunderstanding and violence that dated back to the days of Jamestown, Virginia, and Plymouth Plantation. Coloradans and their native neighbors disagreed on many issues, including who owned the land, how it should be used, and whether they wanted to exist side by side. Many Coloradans had moved west with prejudices against the "noble red man," and they were further antagonized by the fact that the essential overland transportation routes were continually endangered by Indian raids and threats. Rumors circulated that Confederate agents were attempting to stir up trouble by inciting the Plains tribes to raid. But trouble did not come until 1863, when the Sioux, driven out of Minnesota, incensed their Plains cousins, who then directed their retaliation upon the overland trails. Washington rejected Evans's request for federal troops to protect them, absorbed as it was with the more pressing military problem of hammering out victory against the Confederacy.

During the summer and fall, stage stations were raided and wagon trains stopped. The disruption of transportation infuriated Coloradans, who resented the higher prices (their mail from the East had to be routed via San Francisco) and the general interference with their daily lives. Evans attempted to resolve the crisis, but solutions proved elusive. The Indians stopped their attacks when winter came, but the raids were resumed in the spring of 1864. Frustration and anger mounted rapidly. Evans tried unsuccessfully to resolve the conflict in a peaceful manner. When his peace feelers to the tribes were rejected, he turned to raising another regiment of Colorado volunteers. These ninety-day militiamen wanted action, as did most of their Colorado contemporaries. All this hatred and misunderstanding culminated in the infamous attack on Black Kettle's village at Sand Creek on November 29, 1864. The atrocities committed against the Indians that day would besmirch the reputations of Colorado and the individuals involved for years to come.

The immediate result of Sand Creek was to intensify the Indian war and bring about a congressional investigation into that unfortunate event. The long-term consequence was the removal of the Cheyennes and Arapahoes from Colorado's eastern plains. By the late sixties the Indians were gone, and the eastern plains had been opened to the cattleman and the farmer.

All the while, the territory was heating up politically. An offer of statehood was proffered in 1864 when the Republican party, called Union for the war's duration, needed electoral votes. A battle between Denver and the mountain towns, primarily Black Hawk and Central City, ensued. The question of division of the political spoils created much of the controversy, as did jealousy of Denver and its pervasive political greed. The outcome was an unexpected defeat for the statehood party. However, neither the desire for statehood nor the jealousy of Denver had been put to rest; both would return for another round.

Isolation, which the closing of the trails intensified, had not been put to rest, either. The Missouri River and its settlements were a month's travel time to the east by the lumbering freight wagon and five to seven days by a swaying stagecoach. In all other directions stretched open country or small, scattered outposts. The ultimate solution to overcoming the separation — the railroad — would not be a viable option for a few years yet. Coloradans resigned themselves to that fact while holding on to their high hopes that the rails and the steam engine would soon reach them.

Investors were also encouraged to hasten west with desperately needed funds. Placer mining had waned, and in its wake had come hard-rock mining, requiring sophisticated technology, efficient smelting processes, and more money. Coloradans did not have the necessary experience, nor did they have the financial resources to permit a sufficiently heavy concentration of capital. Investment came quite unexpectedly in 1863–64, as the North slogged its way toward victory and its economy hummed as seldom before in American history. Northerners had money to invest and saw the gold mines as good opportunities. Coloradans, who had the gold mines but not the money, were quick to consummate the marriage. Colorado mining stocks, particularly those of Gilpin County, emerged as popular attractions on the New York and other stock exchanges. In their eagerness to promote investment, Coloradans began to describe any hole in the ground as a "promising" mine. The lure of that deception proved irresistible, and easterners in pursuit of that dream of getting rich without working sent their dollars. The unlucky investor saw more of his funds flowing out than in. By April 1864 serious doubts tainted these "mines," and the "gold bubble" burst, leaving Colorado with a tainted reputation in eastern investing circles for over a decade.

The investment frenzy masked another serious problem: the ore being mined could not be refined by methods then available in the territory. All these things dimmed Colorado's mining star while Montana's was rising. That region's new "poor man's diggings" grabbed headlines and pirated Coloradans, much to the dismay of William Byers and other boosters. For the first time, but not the last, Colorado faced a challenge from a mining neighbor.

As the light departed from the haunted landscape of war in 1865, the situation in Colorado, which had looked so promising in 1861, had greatly deteriorated. From under the cloud of the "gold bubble" fiasco, the Sand Creek massacre, the increasingly complex ore-reduction problems, the political turmoil, the unresolved isolation handicap, and a threatening Rocky Mountain rival, Coloradans surveyed the postwar world with trepidation. On top of these obstacles to prosperity came another troubling setback: the transcontinental railroad bypassed the territory, choosing a more northerly route and establishing an urban competitor in Cheyenne, Wyoming, in 1867–68. Some Denver merchants, certain that they saw the handwriting on the wall, packed up and moved to the new metropolis. It was Denver's darkest moment; not even the 1863 fire or 1864 flood was as damaging as this seemingly fatal catastrophe. Fortunately for Denver, city fathers rallied to the challenge and decided to build their own railroad to intersect the transcontinental.

The first train of the Denver Pacific made its run in 1870; before long the Kansas Pacific also chugged into town, giving Denver two rail outlets. The community had become a railroad hub, its future secure, thanks in no small measure to William Byers, John Evans, and others. It would soon be heralded (self-promoted, really) as "Queen of the Mountains and Plains." Cheyenne's threat to its superiority evaporated, defeated by determined local leadership, a better location, and a more economically attractive hinterland.

The coming of the railroad eliminated the most pressing problem of Colorado's first decade: transportation. At the same time, it launched a boom in railroad building that lasted for the next two decades. The state had more miles of track in the late 1890s than at any other time in its history; every community that could possibly gain connections had done so. None of the railroads achieved more fame than the Denver & Rio Grande, the brainchild of William Jackson Palmer. Rather than building east and west, Palmer determined to go south along the foothills to tap the riches of the southern part of the state. Part hardheaded businessman and part idealist, Palmer was first and foremost a railroad man, town builder, and social planner. Colorado Springs and Durango would be his most notable urban accomplishments, while his railroad eventually would open the state's southern and western sections.

The railroads also provided the impetus for developing Colorado's coal fields. Coal had been mined as early as the sixties, but there was no cheap way to transport it. The railroad furnished that method, while also utilizing the coal as fuel; hence, railroad companies came to dominate the initial stages of the industry. The two great fields, the southern (the Walsenburg and Trinidad region) and the northern (Boulder and southwestern Weld counties) were both flourishing by the eighties. Around the mines, company-controlled camps grew up. The life of the coal miner proved to be entirely different from and more dangerous than that of his hard-rock contemporary, a fact that Coloradans did not understand until it was almost too late. As the old saying went, "God made the coal, then he hid it. Then some fool found it and we've been in trouble ever since."

The arrival of the iron horse also spurred growth, and growth brought Colorado nearer to statehood. Territorial status had always frustrated those Coloradans who wanted to be masters of their own fate. They abhorred the fact that Washington had so much say in territorial matters, and some of the political appointments were anathema to them. Not until the mountain towns and Denver temporarily solved their differences and united in a common cause, however, would the statehood movement take wing.

By the mid-seventies national political officials were receptive to the idea. The Republican party needed all the electoral college votes it could muster for the 1876 presidential election. Local and national leaders cooperated to support the election of delegates to the Colorado constitutional convention. The state constitution that resulted was ratified by the voters, and on August 1, 1876, the "Centennial State" joined the union. The state's founding fathers had, however, avoided resolving two controversial questions, leaving them for the state legislature: the location of the capital and whether women should have the right to vote. The latter was decided in 1877 — the male voters said no; the former would not be settled until 1881, when Denver won the designation in a statewide election.

Political advances were matched by advances in mining. Nathaniel Hill, a former Brown University professor of chemistry, had developed a smelting method in the late 1860s that unraveled the refractory-ore puzzle. His Boston and Colorado Smelting Company at Black Hawk was soon handling ores from throughout Colorado and the region, helping to stimulate local mining. The various refining problems intrigued Hill, and his smelter became famous for its scientific approach. When Black Hawk proved too limited a site, he moved his works to the more centrally located and accessible Denver. There Hill helped Colorado emerge as the regional smelting leader.

But the stigma of earlier mining failures continued to plague Colorado unrelentingly. Investors shied way after the "gold bubble" debacle, and without outside investment the territory languished. Even the discovery of mineable amounts of silver in the Georgetown region and across the Snowy Range failed to entice financiers to come back. Discouraged Coloradans found it hard to believe that this, too, would pass. Although silver discoveries at Caribou, tucked away in western Boulder County, ushered in the "silver seventies," still more was needed.

Caribou would beckon for a brief time, and Georgetown for a longer period, but the breakthrough came with the amazing Leadville discoveries in 1877–79. Colorado would rise to become the country's number one mining state, thanks to this new windfall. Since the placer gold excitement of 1860 at Oro City, this isolated corner of Lake County had attracted little interest. Nonetheless, local residents knew there was silver to be had. They needed only financial support and a smelter to start them on what they believed would be the road to prosperity. When major discoveries finally were made on what became Fryer Hill and nearby properties, Oro City was completely eclipsed by Leadville. Colorado's greatest silver strike was destined for the realm of legend. By 1880 well over $11 million worth of silver had come out of its mines, along with $3 million worth of lead. Central City brought a degree of fame and fortune to some, but Leadville made millionaires.

"All roads lead to Leadville," observed author Mary Hallock Foote. She and her mining husband Arthur were two who hurried to the new boomtown. "Everybody was going there! Our fellow citizens as we saw them from the road were more picturesque than pleasing. I was absorbed by this curious exhibition of humanity." After living there for a while, she incisively observed to a friend, "The men out here seem such *boys*, to me — irrespective of age!"

Only Nevada's Comstock Lode and Virginia City rivaled Leadville, and they had already passed their prime. Where investors had once shied away, now they fell over each other to underwrite mines in Leadville and all the other Colorado districts that boosted themselves unblushingly as "the second Leadville." Leadville was indeed legendary, and no legend that grew out of it proved more enduring than that of fifty-niner Horace Tabor. A miner/merchant who came over from Oro City, he became a millionaire within a year and strode with giant steps across the Colorado stage for the next fifteen years. His faith and optimism drove him to reinvest in Colorado, the first of the Colorado millionaire entrepreneurs to do so on such a grand and glorious scale. In the end, his career paralleled that of his beloved mining industry, boom to bust. But this New Englander became the epitome of what Colorado could do for the individual; his was the ultimate success story.

Most success stories took much longer to develop. For example, prospectors and miners had ventured into Colorado's far western corner just before the Leadville excitement and made important discoveries in the craggy, lofty San Juan Mountains. But the recovery of the resources would be forced to await the removal of the Utes, the coming of the railroad, and the infusion of speculators' cash. The wait would be a long one, because first Leadville and then Aspen diverted attention from the region.

The Ute issue was settled within a decade; mining's importance superseded Indian rights when land was involved. Following the classic and tragic pattern so often repeated in the West, the prospectors overran the land in violation of Indian treaty rights, then cried that the Utes must go because they were not utilizing the land or its resources to the best advantage. The Brunot Agreement of 1873 temporarily resolved the dilemma faced by the government, caught as it was between the demands of irate taxpayers and obligations to Indian tribes. The accord opened the mountains to prospecting and mining, but neither side was happy with it and it provided only a temporary truce.

Howls arose from all the San Juan communities and from the mining districts for the removal of the Utes; the idea was supported by many other Coloradans as well. The Utes departed after a well-intentioned but misguided Indian agent, Nathan Meeker, provoked his "wards" into open revolt in 1879. Meeker and other men at his agency were killed, the white women and children were seized, and a column of troops racing to their relief was defeated. The sad story of the Utes climaxed with their being herded onto a reservation in Utah. Only through the persistent, skillful efforts of their most notable leader, Ouray, were the Southern Ute people, who had nothing to do with the Meeker tragedy, allowed to remain on their land along the New Mexico border.

With the Utes removed, the entire Western Slope was opened. In came the Denver & Rio Grande, and settlements at Durango, Montrose, Delta, and Grand Junction soon followed. Ranchers and farmers found the climate and soil much to their liking. The nearby Gunnison country, which had first been prospected at the same time as the San Juans, was also thrown open to miners and settlers. There were hopes that this would be another Leadville, but silver and gold deposits proved small. Fortunately, both hard and soft coal veins were discovered in the Crested Butte area, and ranchers found the mountain valleys attractive for their operations. Settlers swarmed over the Western Slope (except for the northwestern corner) and were soon followed by the Denver & Rio Grande, which in the 1880s managed to tap most of the region. Isolated from their eastern neighbors and relatively powerless politically, the Western Slopers went their independent way beyond the Continental Divide. Colorado, in reality, was not one unified state. Several regions constituted the whole, while the political power was centered upon Denver and its immediate neighbors.

This circumstance created constant envy of the capital city; it was nothing new, just more widespread. Urbanization dominated Colorado during these decades, thanks primarily to mining's urban nature. Denver tripled in size during the decade of the eighties to top 106,000. Leadville silver, continuing dedicated leadership, railroads, and booming environs shot Denver to the top of the regional hierarchy. Pueblo, Colorado Springs, Leadville, Trinidad, and Aspen trailed far behind. On the Western Slope, outside of booming Aspen, Durango was the largest community with 2,700 inhabitants, putting it temporarily ahead of Grand Junction; this side of the mountains would never be as urbanized as the Eastern Slope.

The ebb and flow of mining was already evident in these years. Older communities such as Central City, Georgetown, and Silver Cliff had peaked and declined, while many smaller mining camps quickly deteriorated into ghost towns. Colorado had been fortunate that its mineral treasure box continued to disclose new wonders, unlike some other western mining states that had to rely on one mineral or only a few districts. When the eighties ended, however, most of the state had been prospected, and the question could legitimately be asked how much longer Colorado could rely so much on mining.

Fortunately, new sources of income were already developing. Tourists were on their way, some to see those old mining relics of the past, others to seek the health benefits of the clear, dry Colorado air, and most to enjoy the scenery. Railroads dominated the tourist industry — only the most adventuresome souls dared to leave the security of well-smoothed railroad tracks. Colorado, hailed for years as a health mecca for sufferers of respiratory diseases, became easily accessible once the railroads facilitated travel. They came to Denver, Colorado Springs, and other communities in an attempt to regain their health. Many did improve in the benevolent climate, and the "one-lunged army," as these people were called, became a fixture of the Colorado scene.

Farmers and ranchers also invaded the area when the eastern plains were opened to settlement. Ranchers like John Wesley Iliff arrived first and proved that a profit could be made in the cattle business. After all, the government gave free grass, water, and land; all the individual had to provide were cattle, a branding iron, a home ranch, and some cowboys. Let nature take its course and watch the profits roll in! Eastern and British investors latched onto this new road to wealth and dispatched their money west to multiply. Although the open-range days, as they were called, lasted into the mid-1880s, ranchers never dominated the state as they did in neighboring Wyoming or, to a lesser degree, in Montana.

The farmers moved more slowly, settling along the river bottoms where water was available. The Union Colony, which founded Greeley, was the one major deviation from this pattern. The brainchild of Nathan Meeker and Horace Greeley, the colony pulled together men and families, bought the land, transported the members west, and, most critically, had the finances and wherewithal to develop an irrigation system. By establishing a town and working communally from the start, the Union Colony overcame the problems that usually beset isolated farm families who journeyed west on their own.

Nevertheless, most continued to do just that, migrating because Colorado was touted as the "Garden of Eden." It required some farsighted optimism to envision the "Great American Desert" as a garden. But some theorists argued that rain followed the plow, or that iron rails created electrical currents that "tickled" the rain out of the clouds. The eastern plains were reveling in a wet cycle at the time, so these hypotheses seemed plausible. Whatever one believed seemed enough reason to move west. The farmers' plows turned over the prairie grasses, and their dreams built little villages across the land. So different in spirit, attitudes, and pace from their mountain neighbors, these farm communities also represented their founders' attempts to recreate the life they had left behind. What they lacked in money, investment, publicity, and excitement, they tried to make up for with their determination and positive thinking.

The hopes and dreams of both the ranchers and the farmers came crashing down in the mid- and late eighties. Overcrowding, poor business practices, too much optimism, and fierce winters and dry summers in 1885–86 brought the rancher back down to reality. The farmer soon followed him, a victim of drought, overproduction, and misconceptions about what the soil and climate could support. Settlement receded from the eastern plains; lonely, deserted homesteads and abandoned villages lingered as monuments to exaggerated expectations. But the rancher and the farmer would regroup and try again; they believed this reversal to be merely a temporary snag.

To most Coloradans, however, the problems of the plains seemed remote. The 1880s were the silver decade. When Leadville production peaked and leveled, Aspen rushed in to reign as the new "silver queen." Increasing production in the San Juans and other regions also served to maintain Colorado's position as a major mining state. Even Gilpin County and Central City contributed their share of wealth, mostly in gold. The production of coal expanded, as did that of the base metals. Furthermore, Colorado kept its status as the smelting hub of the Rocky Mountains; both Denver and Pueblo had some of the country's most modern facilities. Pueblo was at that time emerging as a center of iron and steel production and had designs on becoming the "Pittsburgh of the West."

All in all, Colorado's economy looked more prosperous and more balanced than it ever had before. Mining still dominated, but agriculture, industry, and tourism each contributed a growing share to the state's economic health. The frontier days, now a generation removed, were already being honored in fact and myth. The frontier was a time and a way of life, never a place; the Colorado frontier had passed, but it endured in its people, the fifty-niners and their contemporaries. They had already converted into legends the things they wanted to believe about what had happened in their lifetimes.

The frontier phase had evaporated in the twinkling of an eye; mining had seen to that. Urbanization came hard on the heels of the miners and with it business, culture, and all the trimmings. These pioneers had striven from the start to recreate the best of the lives they had left behind, whether at the old home place in Illinois, New York, or Cornwall, England. Schools had been established, followed by institutions of higher education. Theaters, often called opera houses, were hosts to the newest plays and the classics as well. Thanks to Horace Tabor, Denver erected the finest opera house between St. Louis and San Francisco, and it did produce operas.

Literary clubs, bands, and a wide variety of societies and fraternal groups took root to try to overcome the early rootlessness of the settlers and to provide a taste of home. Preachers arrived with the fifty-niners, and churches were not far behind, bringing spiritual values to temper the materialism that dominated the era in the Rockies and across the United States. Baseball was born in 1860, and by the seventies most Colorado communities had town teams to uphold their honor.

Colorado had taken major strides in the generation since the Pike's Peak rush. The region had been explored, opened, developed, and settled. A transportation network, featuring the narrow-gauge track that Palmer had pioneered, tied the Eastern and Western slopes together, as well as all the major cities. The economy, initially based on mining alone, had developed a mixture of industries that would contribute to its success in the next century. A walk down the main street of a mining town or some of the communities nestled along the foothills would reveal just how much the business and professional communities had diversified. Doctors, lawyers, and dentists rubbed elbows with grocers, druggists, bankers, photographers, and saloon keepers. Where newspapers had

once been rare, now almost every town of any size had one, and the larger ones several. They promoted, praised, defended, feuded, reformed, and served as local gadflies.

Overall, Colorado had done remarkably well in thirty years. Certainly there had been periods of economic stagnation, and some developments had hindered rather than helped Colorado's progress, but these appeared to have been overcome. The state's dependence upon externally established economic values for mineral and agricultural products created two facts of life for Coloradans. First, outside economic forces would be a vital influence on their lives; second, there would be inevitable cycles of boom and bust over which they could exercise little control.

Coloradans were able to look ahead with optimism to the 1890s; only a few clouds darkened their skies. As William Byers had written on that glorious August 1, 1876: "Three Cheers for the State of Colorado . . . a sovereign state, mistress of herself and her destinies, Colorado will now conquering, and to conquer, pursue the path of prosperity."

It had been an exciting generation. A time of joys and a time of sorrows, it had been most of all a time of unlimited possibilities. For many, Colorado was seen as the promised land. Neither the people, nor the land they overran, would ever be the same again.

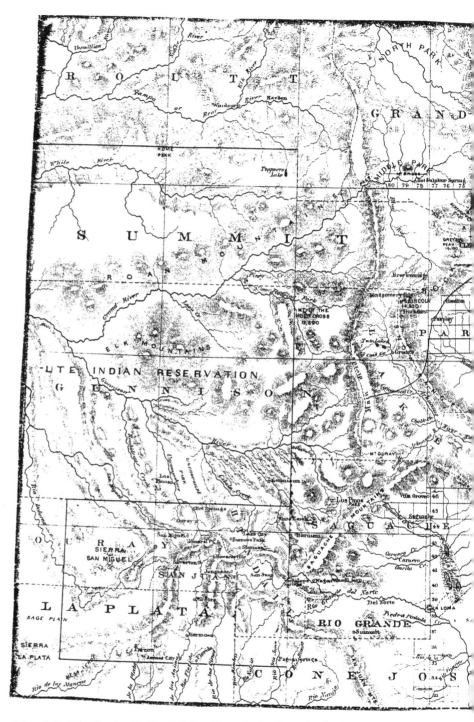

Colorado in 1876. *Courtesy Fort Lewis College/Center for Southwest Studies, Durango.*

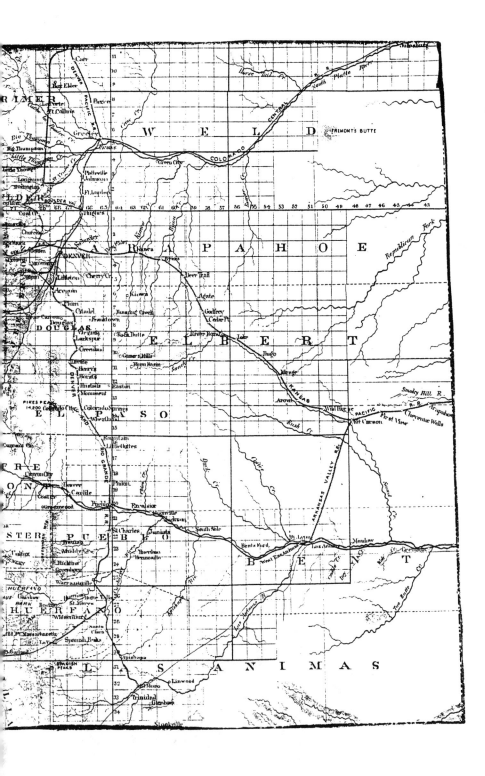

Steely-eyed William Bent was a major figure in the fur and hide trade. Bent, his brother Charles, and Ceran St. Vrain formed a company that built Bent's Fort on the Arkansas River. Charles was appointed governor of New Mexico in 1846. William married into the Cheyenne tribe and had several mixed-blood sons. *Courtesy Colorado Historical Society, Denver.*

Mountain man Jim Beckworth's mother was a slave. Beckworth went to the mountains in 1824 with William Ashley and later trapped with men such as Tom Fitzpatrick, Thomas "Peg Leg" Smith, and Louis Vasquez before settling in Denver. Later he guided John Chivington to Sand Creek and was appalled by the massacre of Cheyennes. *Courtesy Colorado Historical Society, Denver.*

Charles Stobie, D. C. Oakes, and Jim Baker. Baker journeyed to the mountains with the American Fur Company in 1838; he was associated with Jim Bridger and later settled in the vicinity of Denver. A guide and interpreter for Ute agent D. C. Oakes in 1865, Baker moved to the Little Snake Valley in the 1870s. Oakes wrote a glowing popular guidebook in 1858 and received a good deal of criticism from disappointed fifty-niners. Stobie came to Colorado in 1865, lived with the Utes for a time, and helped Oakes, Baker, and others locate the White River Ute Agency. *Courtesy Colorado Historical Society, Denver.*

"Pike's Peak or Bust!" One hundred thousand people, give or take a few, started for the "new Eldorado" in 1859. Discouraged by reports of a humbug, about half turned back before reaching Denver. This wagon is at St. Joseph, Missouri, four weeks away from the gold fields. *Courtesy Kansas State Historical Society, Topeka.*

In the scramble to "get rich without working," little attention was paid to mining's impact on the land. This early 1860s scene is in Gilpin County, where placer mining soon gave way to hard-rock mining. *Courtesy Denver Public Library/Western History Department.*

First territorial governor William Gilpin ran afoul of his fears that Southerners would subvert Coloradans. He helped raise the First Colorado Regiment but did not bask in its 1862 glories. Gilpin remained in Colorado after his removal from office and became revered as a pioneer. *Courtesy Colorado Historical Society, Denver.*

Empire, near the foot of Berthoud Pass, was one of Civil War Colorado's important mining districts. A recruiting squad of the First Colorado is drumming up business in this 1861 photo. The district gradually declined after the war; tourism eventually replaced mining as the basis of the local economy. *Courtesy Colorado Historical Society, Denver.*

George Bent and his wife, Magpie, 1867. Bent was the son of William Bent and Owl Woman of the Cheyennes. Magpie was the niece of the famous Cheyenne Chief Black Kettle. Magpie's dress is elkskin with elk teeth and was in her family for some 200 years. *Courtesy Colorado Historical Society, Denver.*

A fire on April 19, 1863, and this flood of May 20, 1864, failed to stop Denver's march toward regional dominance. While Denverites inspected the damage, planning for the future was already under way. Even being bypassed by the transcontinental railroad did not undermine the local leadership's determination. *Photo by George Wakeley. Courtesy Colorado Historical Society, Denver.*

John Chivington (ca. 1864), Methodist preacher and military leader, gained fame in both fields. The Sand Creek massacre in November 1864 ruined his reputation. *Courtesy Colorado Historical Society, Denver.*

The Cheyennes and Arapahoes lived on the eastern plains. Sometimes they warred with the Mountain Utes. Their way of life was doomed by the 1859 rush. Sadly, whites and Indians never tried to understand each other, and tragedy followed. The Plains tribes gave way by the late sixties. *Courtesy Denver Public Library/Western History Department.*

A group of Utes at the Los Pinos Agency near Cochetopa Pass. This group went to Washington, D.C., following the Brunot Agreement in 1873. Ouray and Chipeta are seated in the front row (center); Otto Mears is in the middle row (far right). *Courtesy Denver Public Library/Western History Department.*

The haunting look of a Plains woman caught between two cultures. She and her people lost their land and way of life. *Courtesy Denver Public Library/Western History Department.*

The famous Ute leader Ouray and his wife, Chipeta, in the 1860s. He tried hard to keep his people at peace with their neighbors, but the crush of settlement proved too great, and by the early 1880s all except the Southern Utes were gone from Colorado. *Courtesy La Plata County Historical Society, Durango.*

Plains tribes that roamed through eastern Colorado included the Cheyennes, Arapahoes, Sioux, and others. Many Sioux joined the Cheyennes after the Sand Creek massacre in 1864. Spotted Fawn (above) was a Sioux. *Courtesy Fort Collins Public Library*.

The Utes came to Durango to trade and camped diagonally across from the Strater, Durango's finest nineteenth-century hotel. Eastern tourists found the "old West" at their doorstep. *Courtesy Amon Carter Museum, Fort Worth.*

The Hayden Survey was one of the major federal explorations of Colorado. Its 1873–76 expeditions left behind a rich heritage of photographs and reports, as well as a variety of other information. *Photo by William Henry Jackson. Courtesy U.S. Geological Survey, Denver.*

Fort Garland (pictured in 1874) defended the southern San Luis Valley before the Pike's Peak rush. Established in 1858, it continued as a post until 1883. Its troops were involved in several campaigns against the Utes. *Courtesy Colorado Historical Society, Denver.*

Del Norte was a gateway for miners going to the San Juans by way of treacherous Stony Pass and on to Silverton. This group of wagons, including one with a boiler, prepared to leave Del Norte in 1877. *Courtesy Colorado Historical Society, Denver.*

An eight-mule team driven by Andy Woodruff. David Wood, the owner, was a major freighter in western Colorado both before and after the railroad appeared. Wood's wagons carried everything from fine china to heavy mining equipment. *Courtesy Museum of Western Colorado, Grand Junction.*

Yampa and Kremmling stage headed east with Tommy Cole driving and Mrs. Hooper on top. Stages first appeared in 1859 and were still carrying passengers after the turn of the century. *Courtesy Grand County Museum, Hot Sulphur Springs.*

Colorado mines were perched near mountain tops and in valley floors. This mine was located in the Red Mountain district of the San Juans, where silver was the cry in the 1880s. *Courtesy Ouray County Historical Society.*

Prospectors searched for the ore; miners like these dug it out of the ground. It was a hard, dangerous life for $3 a day, minus room and board, as these San Juan miners well knew. *Courtesy Ouray County Historical Society.*

Starting with Nathaniel Hill's Black Hawk operation, smelters became familiar features of Colorado mining. They polluted the atmosphere and endangered workers and nearby residents. This is the Arkansas Valley Smelter at Leadville, ca. 1880. *Photo by Brisbois. Courtesy Mining Gallery, Leadville.*

Leadville was a magic town in the late 1870s and early 1880s. In this photograph from that era, a "jack train" gets ready to haul supplies to an isolated mine or a smaller mining camp nearby. *Photo by Brisbois. Courtesy Mining Gallery, Leadville.*

The Chinese were not often welcomed in Colorado mining districts. They were considered harbingers of decline. This Chinese placer mining operation was located at Gold Hill, one of the original 1859 gold discoveries. *Courtesy Colorado College/Special Collections, Colorado Springs.*

The merchant was a familiar figure in Colorado's mining camps and towns. David May went on to establish a retail empire in Denver. Irwin (also known as Ruby Camp), the community shown here, fared less well, lasting only a little over five years; by 1883 its day had passed. *Courtesy Colorado Historical Society, Denver.*

Bringing out the dead from Woodstock, 1884. Woodstock was a silver camp north of Monarch Pass and east of Pitkin and Ohio City. On March 10, 1884, an avalanche destroyed the town and killed most of the small camp's residents. A train approaching the Alpine Tunnel set off the avalanche by blowing its whistle. *Courtesy Frontier Historical Society, Glenwood Springs.*

Construction of the North St. Vrain road between Lyons and Estes Park, ca. 1875. *Courtesy Estes Park Historical Museum.*

The initial run of water in the Main Street lateral in Greeley, 1870. The first major Colorado irrigation project took place here, and the success of the Union Colony inspired many similar efforts. None proved as successful. *Courtesy City of Greeley Museums.*

Railroading in Colorado was a technological wonder. This is the Silverton Railroad's Corkscrew Gulch turntable. Track mileage reached its peak in Colorado in the 1890s. *Courtesy Fort Lewis College/Center of Southwest Studies, Durango.*

Railroads played a major role in the development of Colorado's mining regions. Here Otto Mears, pioneer road builder, stands by the cowcatcher and engine #100 on the Silverton Railroad. *Courtesy Denver Public Library/Western History Department.*

Cowboys at dinner in southwestern Colorado. The size of the crew indicates that this was roundup time. *Photo by J. J. Carpenter. Courtesy University of Colorado/Western Historical Collections, Boulder.*

Haying in Moraine Park in 1885. Crops were limited in these high-country meadows. Eventually this valley became part of Rocky Mountain National Park. *Courtesy Estes Park Historical Museum.*

Officers of the Prairie Cattle Company in its Trinidad office, 1886: Murdo McKenzie (center), Mr. Johnson (behind McKenzie), W. J. Todd (right), Mr. Hopkins (left). Cattle companies were important in Colorado and elsewhere in the West, attracting eastern and European capital to the frontier. McKenzie, a Scot, also was involved in the giant Matador Cattle Company. *Courtesy Denver Public Library/Western History Department.*

This was the entire population of Walden in 1887. The town was founded two years earlier as a supply point for ranches and farms in North Park, one of the most isolated regions in Colorado. Here the Greene, Rathbun, and Shippey families gather before recently constructed homes. *Courtesy Colorado Historical Society, Denver.*

Many a lonely cowboy or miner fantasized over nudes such as this. Others looked at the paintings hanging in their favorite saloons. *Courtesy Strater Hotel, Durango.*

Fire department in La Junta. Companies such as this one were social organizations, sponsoring dances and other public affairs. *Courtesy Denver Public Library/Western History Department.*

Aunt Clara Brown, an ex-slave, became a legend in her own day in Central City, where she was one of the first settlers. She eventually moved to Denver and died there in 1885. *Photo by Green and Cancannon. Courtesy Colorado Historical Society, Denver.*

Amazon guards, an auxiliary to Company F of the state militia under Tom Crawford in Grand Junction, was an example of a small-town social organization, ca. 1880s. *Courtesy Museum of Western Colorado, Grand Junction.*

The Colorado Springs Police Department in 1887. It was rare to have a black policeman in the nineteenth century. Two of the big problems for any force were drunks and dogs. *Courtesy Colorado Springs Pioneers Museum.*

Trinidad, Commercial Street, 1889. A supply center and coal town, Trinidad dates from 1859; earlier, the site was a rendezvous for trappers and traders. *Courtesy Carnegie Library, Trinidad.*

II

NEVER TO COME BACK TO THEM
1890–1914

COLORADO EMBARKED UPON THE 1890s in much the same way as it had every previous decade, with optimism and what seemed to be a bright future. The few problems that lingered were seen as only minor threats, which another rich mining discovery would easily dispose of. Several years had passed, however, since any such event had created a boom.

Coloradans had their wish granted for one more excitement. This time it came from southwest of Pike's Peak. No gold had been found there back in 1859 even though the rush had been named after that prominent geographic landmark. A woebegone prospector/cowboy, Bob Womack, had searched the area for years without noticeable success; then in 1890 he opened a claim assayed at $250 in gold per ton of ore. Within a year a district called Cripple Creek had been organized — the rush was on.

Silver had dominated Colorado mining for two decades; gold now surged back to the forefront. The district produced $557,000 (at $20 per ounce) in 1892 and a decade's high of over $16 million in 1899. Not until 1918 would production dip under $10 million per year. Cripple Creek yielded more gold than had ever been mined before in Colorado and proved a worthy rival to California's mother lode country. Irony lay in the fact that the dreams of the fifty-niners would finally be fulfilled a generation later within the shadow of their rush's namesake, Pike's Peak.

Once again the eager fortune hunters rushed in, finding that these gold-bearing lodes ran contrary to previous Colorado veins and outcrops. The amateur could do as well as the expert in this new game of finding the paying claim. One longtime prospector who played the game exceptionally well was Winfield Scott Stratton, for whom Cripple Creek literally became the pot of gold. Stratton had moved through most of Colorado — Leadville, Silverton, Silver Cliff, Ouray — with no success. At last this part-time Colorado Springs carpenter hit it big. His Independence Mine made him a millionaire several times over before he sold it in 1899 for $10 million, the highest price paid for a Colorado mine up to that time. In his own way, he became what Horace Tabor had been earlier: a legend in his own time.

Around the mines, towns and camps blossomed: Cripple Creek, Victor, Goldfield, Altman, Elkton, names that conjured visions of wealth for a new generation of newspaper readers and investors. Thirty years of growth and development since the 1860s had swiftly dispatched the primitiveness that characterized those earlier days. Electric lights, telephones, newspapers, churches, schools, chambers of commerce, stock exchanges — they all appeared almost immediately. Harry Newman wrote excitedly to his future wife, "This is the only country to live in and make money."

The railroads lost no time either; they brought the tourists in to see the sights almost before the sights were seeable. Mabel Barbee Lee remembered the day the first train arrived: "What bedlam broke loose! Hysterical men and women shrieked and yelled and hugged each other for joy. Bombs and pistol shots added to the pandemonium." Interested observers hastened to see it all before the passing of the old West eliminated their chance to observe it firsthand. The prevailing philosophy was, "You can wait around and hope but you'll never see the likes of this again."

The bellwether of the district, the town of Cripple Creek, gave them everything they wanted to see. Its population was reported to be 5,000 in 1893, and the census takers counted over 10,000 in 1900. Victor, nearer the major mines and characterized as a working man's community, was never able to match its rival in either reputation, population, or wealth, but it grew to nearly 5,000.

There was, and always had been, a darker side to all the wonders that were immediately evident. The editor of the *Cripple Creek Crusher* had written on December 2, 1892, that "greed and avarice are regarded as prime motives of life in a mining camp." He was supporting an attempt to ensure that all the "little ones" received gifts that Christmas. Newman complained three years later that it was impossible to find a room; the town was so crowded that rents had gone up by five dollars, and then ten more dollars, in the past month. Working in the mines was perilous, as Anne Ellis found out. A delegation of her husband's co-workers came to inform her that he had drilled into a missed hole. "But — well, Ma'am, you might as well know," they sadly told her. "He is dead, shot all to pieces."

Although the exhilaration of Cripple Creek overshadowed all else, the San Juans finally came into their own in the nineties. Having secured railroad connections at last and now attracting investors and publicity (Creede's silver stampede came at the same time as Cripple Creek's), the San Juan district at last realized its promised potential. The Telluride-Ouray-Silverton triangle harbored major gold deposits, not to mention the silver that had been mined for years. Thus, Colorado was doubly blessed as the decade moved along. Older districts, such as Central City, Georgetown, and Leadville, continued to produce $1 million to $2 million worth of metals annually. Though not bad for such thoroughly worked-over districts, their output paled in comparison to that of the other booming two.

Colorado's cup seemed to overflow, but it was about to spring a leak. The problem came from silver, the price of which had collapsed from $1.25 to the 90-cents-per-ounce range by the 1890s. And that was for the refined product — mine owners received less for the raw material. The lowered value of silver, prevalent for almost two decades and the bane of all silver producers, would not go away. It became known as the "silver issue." Before it ran its course, every Coloradan, young and old, would hear of it, and most would rue the day it reared its head.

Coloradans liked to say that the issue arose from the "Crime of '73," which, in practical terms, meant that gold dollars were to be used as the basic unit of value in place of silver dollars. Contrary to the claims of later silverites, this action had been no diabolical plot concocted by the "gold bugs" to push their currency to prominence. It simply reflected an economic fact of life: the price of silver on the commercial market (over $1.30 an ounce) was higher than the mint was allowed to pay by law, that being a sixteen-to-one value-ratio of gold to silver. The price of gold was pegged internationally at $20 an ounce, making the government's top price for silver $1.25, well below the going market rate. Unable to find suppliers willing to sell at its price, the government simply stopped coining silver in 1873.

This action received very little attention at the time, because miners were making money on the open market. In the years that followed, the circumstances changed dramatically. New silver discoveries in the Rocky Mountain states and in Nevada flooded the market with silver bullion. A number of European countries, including Germany and France, adopted the gold standard and discontinued silver currency. The combination of reduced demand and increased production caused the price of silver to drop to an average of $1.12 by 1879.

Miners now sought to sell to the treasury at $1.25 an ounce, only to find out, much to their dismay, that the government was not in the market for silver.

The silver men protested that the Crime of '73 deprived them of their opportunity to sell their silver at a profit and at an amount above the world metal price. Therein lay the basis of the silver issue. It took but an instant for the silverites to see it as a plot by the gold advocates. The easiest solution, as the silverites saw it, was to persuade the government to start purchasing silver again at the old sixteen-to-one ratio.

Those directly involved in silver mines (owners, managers, and miners) and those dependent on silver mines in less direct ways (smelter men, railroad men and suppliers) raised the silver banner. The silver issue affected virtually all Coloradans in some way; consequently, much of the population hastened to join the crusade. Other silver-producing western states and territories fell into line and brought pressure to bear on Washington. The "ruthless" Crime of '73 was angrily lambasted, and Congress was lobbied for relief. From the point of view of Coloradans, a simple goal emerged involving two things: resumption of the government's purchase of silver and a guaranteed price. Results came quickly. Over President Rutherford Hayes's veto and the objections of those who believed silver was inflationary, Congress passed the Bland-Allison Act of 1878. The act met the silver champions partway, but as a compromise it satisfied neither side. The bill authorized the treasury to purchase between $2 million and $4 million worth of silver per month and provided for the bullion's coinage into silver dollars. The government would pay the same price as that offered on the current world market. The price temporarily stabilized, then retreated again and continued to slip as Leadville and Aspen silver hit the market.

Colorado, now the number one silver state, was infuriated with this "half-loaf," particularly because the treasury purchased only the minimum amount allowable. Thus, the demand for free coinage of silver did not die. Instead it gained momentum as the decade of the eighties ran out.

Silver became the touchstone for Colorado politics — to have a chance at election, a candidate had to be foursquare behind silver. Emotion replaced logic on every front. Beloved U.S. Senator Henry Teller stated emphatically that "silver is adapted by nature to supply the wants of the human race as money." Colorado newspapers argued that "silver has become the symbol of revolt against the centralized 'money power' Wall Street and the European exchanges." Denver's *Weekly Tribune-Republican* warned its readers that if silver continued to decline, mines would suspend work and "hundreds of thousands of men would be thrown out of employment" (August 5, 1886). Silver Plume's *Silver Standard* called the conflict a "war" on June 24, 1896, and summoned its readers to "carry on the fight in the enemy's stronghold [the East]." Silver,

Horace Tabor claimed, was "the money of the constitution"; the free coinage of both gold and silver had been the founding fathers' legacy. Others referred to silver and gold as the money of the Bible.

Coloradans were becoming radical in defense of their basic, conservative interests. They organized silver clubs and a silver association, held national silver conventions, and spread the gospel as far afield as possible. Their appeal was heard by another hard-pressed group, the farmers, who encountered their own economic woes because of overproduction, declining prices, and mounting debts. Colorado farmers listened with interest as the silverites promised higher prices and expanded markets for farm products once silver resumed its rightful place in the monetary system. The plan sounded reasonable as it was presented. Desperation became the mother of overzealous hope. Thus it was that the "cause" spread beyond the mines and the mining towns.

Politics and silver also joined forces in other mining states. State and national spokesmen of both parties consistently championed bimetallism—that is, a return to silver coinage. They lobbied diligently in Washington without success, even with support from western colleagues and from enthusiastic inflationists. This latter group was convinced that silver would do what its long-championed paper-money plans had failed to accomplish: bring about a more flexible money supply and inflation. Eastern bankers, businessmen, and monied men overwhelmingly opposed the idea on all counts, and through their handmaidens, the Republican party and the financial press, they hammered away at such heresies.

In 1890 a breakthrough was finally achieved with the passage of the Sherman Silver Purchase Act, another "half-loaf" victory for the silverites. Passed in return for western support for the McKinley Tariff Act, the Sherman Act required the government to buy 4.5 million ounces of silver per month, roughly the amount produced in the United States at that time. Colorado, which produced 58 percent of the silver mined domestically each year, applauded when the price jumped from 94 cents to $1.05. Alas, the hope proved illusory, and the bottom fell out of the market. The government was required to purchase only at the market price — nothing more was guaranteed — and the market price dropped to 65 cents an ounce in 1894. Hence, the Sherman Silver Purchase Act delivered no magic elixir.

During this time, another champion arose on the horizon: the People's party, better known as the Populist party. Broad-based disenchantment with the national policies of the Republican and Democratic parties gave this new party a foothold on the political scene. The Populists entered the fray in 1891 and ran a full ticket in Colorado the next year. This was a reform party, providing an alternative to the "two peas in the same pod" philosophies of the traditional parties. It advocated a graduated income tax, a system of postal savings banks, the eight-hour day for labor, the Australian secret ballot, government ownership and operation of railroads, telegraph and telephone systems, and the return of political power to the people through the ballot initiative, referendum, and direct election of U.S. senators. Most important from Coloradans' perspective was the Populists' support for the free and unlimited coinage of silver at the sixteen-to-one ratio. Conservatives of both parties were horrified by what they perceived as a call for revolution; agrarians, western miners, and their supporters saw it as a long overdue cry for independence.

The Populist movement swept Colorado in the 1892 election. Populist presidential candidate James Weaver carried the state, and the party won both congressional seats, the governorship and, with the aid of the silver Democrats, the Colorado senate. The Republicans held on to the state assembly by a one-vote majority. The year of the jubilee seemed to be at hand; Colorado and the Populist party would lead the way to the silver millennium.

But Colorado was not destined to be a one-issue state in those turbulent days of the 1890s. The mining community may have been patriotically united behind free silver, but on the other pressing issue facing it — unionism — it was decidedly fractured. Over the years the proudly independent nature of the hard-rock miner had been eroded. The growth of corporate control and absentee ownership, accompanied by the decline of individual opportunity, augured changes for the hard-rock mines. By the late 1880s miners had become laborers in industrial America, employed in a dangerous, difficult job for someone else's profit, at wages prescribed by management. Opportunities were no longer available to "go down the hill" to a new, booming district when working conditions and pay rates did not meet expectations. The circle of life was closing in on the hard-rock miner; indeed, Cripple Creek was the only mecca left by the early 1890s. As a result, Colorado, which had been generally free of labor strife, descended into two decades of struggle that left their mark on the state for a generation.

The miners' situation elsewhere in the West was little better. In an effort to improve their lot, the miners sent representatives to Butte, Montana, in 1893 to form the Western Federation of Miners. Coloradans joined forces with the rest, and local organizations soon sprang up in the state. Owners and managers were aghast at what, to them, was un-American activity. Unions, they believed, deprived the workers of the right to sell their services in a free job market, curbed business's right to manage its property, and trailed a violent reputation. From the miners' point of view, the WFM held out great promise for achieving collective action and broader powers. The union supported, among other things, better wages, safety and health laws, child labor laws, and the "unlimited coinage" of silver and gold. The miners promised in their preamble to "use all honorable means to maintain friendly relations between ourselves and our employers," then concluded by stating that one of their goals was "to procure employment for our members in preference to non-union men." That last item confirmed the worst fears of the owners, and the battle lines were drawn in all the major districts throughout the state.

The Populists, the WFM, and Coloradans in general were not prepared, however, for what hit them in that tumultuous year of 1893 — the worst economic crash in the nation's history. Almost immediately, the state slipped into a decline that lingered for years. Of all the states, Colorado appeared to be the hardest hit, especially when the government's repeal of the Sherman Silver Purchase Act forced one mine after another to shut down. Depression stalked the land.

With one notable exception, the causes of the panic and crash were familiar — agricultural woes, overexpansion in industry, shaky world business conditions, and collapsing stock prices. The unusual factor revolved around the federal treasury. Businessmen and others assumed that as long as there was $100 million in gold in the treasury, the gold standard was sound and the government would remain solvent. For nearly twenty years there had been no cause to worry, but in April 1893 the gold reserve dropped below that figure and panic set in. While this depletion was caused by a variety of factors, eastern sound-money men blamed the Sherman Silver Purchase Act. Vigorously determined to maintain the gold standard, President Grover Cleveland called a special session of Congress to repeal the obnoxious act. Over the emotional objections of Senator Henry Teller and others, the deed was accomplished. The price of silver plummeted, and Colorado experienced the worst depression in its memory. A dozen Denver banks failed in July, leaving depositors who did not retrieve their money before the doors closed holding empty savings bags; no federal insurance came to the rescue. By September, 150 businesses had failed, and the capital city's situation was called "depressing." Reports from other communities were no better. From Washington County: "The situation in our vicinity is indeed gloomy. The death of silver is the death of farming in this state." From Mesa County: "seventy per cent of the farmers of this valley are mortgaged beyond the possibility of redemption unless our mining industry is revived." From Pitkin County: "The situation is bad and couldn't be very much worse. If we get no favorable legislation, Aspen and vicinity is a goner."

The Colorado Bureau of Labor Statistics found that during July and August over 45,000 persons had lost their jobs and 435 mines had closed. But statistics and words cannot tell the whole story. As businesses, mines, and mills closed, employees were thrown out of work. Those who kept their jobs faced salary cuts; with a larger labor pool available, employers could easily replace dissatisfied workers. The unemployed converged upon Denver; its overburdened charities soon ran out of money and were forced to limit aid. The federal government did nothing; as in past depressions, it believed its responsibility was to remain solvent and let business take care of the economic woes. Populist Governor Davis Waite, determined to resort to "home remedies," summoned a special session of the legislature. Little came of it except a few modifications of the state laws regarding debts and interest. A scheme to coin silver dollars did nothing but attract eastern derision.

Cripple Creek and its gold glowed as the only bright spot, but even there trouble exploded in 1894. Miners flocked to it from the foundering silver districts; where else was there to turn? With a growing labor surplus in their favor, some Cripple Creek mine owners moved to reduce wages from the standard $3 per day to $2.50, or, as an alternative, to increase the workday from eight to ten hours at the old wages. High living costs in the new district were hurting the miners, even at $3 per day; at less than that the outlook turned grim. They joined the WFM in large numbers, and the two groups glared ominously at each other.

In January a group of owners unilaterally decided to institute the nine-hour, $3 day. The union went out on strike, and by the end of February most of the Cripple Creek mines and many of the smelters had shut down. Threats and pressure did not budge the miners; both sides organized small armies, and combatants were roughed up. Waite, who had just finished a well-publicized "war" to clean up Denver's Police and Fire Board, sent in the National Guard to quell the disturbances. The old reformer backed the miners, much to the owners' chagrin, and the WFM won; the eight-hour day and the $3 wage were restored. The union cheered, its membership soared, and it looked as if a new day had dawned for miners. The owners retrenched, waited for another round, and vowed to capture the governor's chair with a pro-business candidate.

The costs in lost wages, production, state expenses, and bitterness were high, and this was just the beginning of a twenty-year confrontation. Waite would be defeated in 1894, succeeded by a long line of governors who favored business; the owners had learned their lessons well. When the next strike broke out, in Leadville in 1896, they demonstrated just how well. This time they were unified, having organized an association; they fortified their properties and brought in strikebreakers. Eventually they called for the National Guard, which marched in to support management. The strike dragged on for months. But the owners were stronger; the miners finally conceded and dejectedly returned to work on their employers' terms. The WFM gained neither recognition nor the restoration of the pre-1893 wage scale. It was now a battle to the death that both sides were determined to win.

Amid the general gloom of 1893, women gained the right to vote. The issue had come up before at the time of the writing of the state constitution, but the founding fathers opted for political expediency and passed the hot issue on to the first legislature. In 1877 the legislators put the proposal before the voters, who rejected it. Colorado thereupon lost the opportunity to be the first state to award suffrage to women (Wyoming was first, in 1890).

In the years that followed, the percentage of women slowly grew in this once largely masculine world, and their influence increased even more dramatically. By 1890 the state was home to 167,000 women (two and a half times the 1880 total), 40 percent of Colorado's population. Working through churches, they helped reform their home communities and smooth the rough edges of society. They organized clubs and libraries, worked for better schools, and accomplished a host of other things that made life in Colorado more like the lives they had left behind. In so doing they also sharpened their leadership and organizational skills. Some professional and business doors that stayed closed to their sisters in the East were opened to them. In the 1890s, with the Populist movement's spirit of reform in the air, they organized the Colorado Equal Suffrage Association, one of the most effective women's organizations ever to operate in the state.

Sixty suffrage chapters and 10,000 women were working for "equal rights and justice for all" in 1893. Editorial support, political and labor endorsements, efficient organization, and careful campaigning paid off handsomely. Colorado men endorsed women's suffrage by over 6,000 votes in November, and the state became the second to allow women to vote. It was a milestone in the women's movement, but only two other states followed suit in the next decade. In fact, it was debated for the next decade whether Colorado and women had actually accrued any benefits from this progressive step. As late as 1903 two reporters for national magazines came to opposite conclusions. "The possession of the ballot, and the employment of that possession, have hurt the women of Colorado as women can least afford to be hurt. Her ideals have been lowered; the delicacy of her perception of right and wrong has been dulled," claimed one. But another opined that women's access to the ballot "forced political parties to put cleaner men on tickets" and added dignity to politics. The issue would have to be debated elsewhere; Colorado had made its choice.

Although they could not vote for the president, women were able to involve themselves in one of the most exciting campaigns in Colorado history, the election of 1896. The election revolved around the free silver issue, which took on new urgency after the crash of 1893. Colorado was ready to revolt, along with its western neighbors.

The Republicans nominated William McKinley for president and pledged themselves to the gold standard; Republican fortunes, which had not fared well in Colorado for several years, hit rock bottom, and the party's stranglehold on the state ended. The Democrats selected William Jennings Bryan and free silver (as well as most of the Populist platform) to carry their banner. According to the July 11 edition of the *Rocky Mountain News*, Bryan embodied the "new order of things, new issues, new men, new geographical groupings." "Our Religion! Silver First, Politics Last," cried the *Mancos Times* (September 11, 1896). The "Battle of the Standards" was vigorously waged, although there was no question where Colorado's heart lay. Mining engineer James D. Hague, on his way to visit the Tomboy Mine, wrote his wife in November, "In Colorado Bryan is regarded as a Moses, a divinely appointed leader of the people, or, at least, a Lincoln, raised up to save and redeem his people." Bryan captured over 85 percent of the vote (he was nominated by both the Democrats and the Populists), winning in La Plata County, for example, 2,729 to 88; in Pitkin County, 3,020 to 30; and on the entire Western Slope, 11,888 to 407.

Both free silver and Colorado hopes were dashed when McKinley carried enough of the other states to win. Coloradans were stunned by the outcome, but their lives went on, their disappointment eased by the Cripple Creek bonanza and the slow improvement of the state's economy. Silver as a national issue died that year, and so did the Populist party, although many of the reforms it advocated were adopted by the Democrats.

In the fast-paced days of the nineties, one issue was hardly buried before another arose. This time it was Cuba, and the ramifications of Manifest Destiny and America's emerging role on the world scene. Coloradans, like other Americans, naively watched the developments that ultimately led to war with Spain in April 1898. Then they blithely marched off to what they called a "splendid little war," which was concluded by August. Very few understood the total impact of what had happened so quickly and so easily. America had acquired an empire, a fact brought home to Colorado when more boys died fighting to "save our little brown brother" from himself in the Philippines (and to hold on to the new empire) than died in the war to liberate Cuba, the Philippines, and other places from Spain. This particular action held more diplomatic and national implications for the new century than most Americans realized at the time.

The twentieth century rushed in like a lion for Colorado. The depression limped off into the sunset, forgotten amid the labor strikes that rocked the state for fourteen years. The issues were old — management versus labor, recognition of the union, control of the district — but the battle was more hostile, both sides being more belligerent than ever before. Giant corporations became more dominant, a trend illustrated no more clearly than by the emergence of the American Smelting and Refining Company. This New Jersey conglomerate gained control of the major smelters in Colorado and many of the largest plants across the country.

Labor trouble erupted in Telluride in 1901 when the San Juans boomed as never before. A compromise was reached, only to unravel two years later when strikes rocked both of the remaining major mining districts. At Cripple Creek and Telluride, the patterns were distressingly similar — clashing goals, breakdown of talks, strikes, violence, calls for the National Guard, martial law, violation of civil rights, and finally the triumph of mine owners. There was no peace for the districts or the state. In the end everyone lost — the union, management, the state, and Coloradans. The unrest exacted a tremendous cost in human suffering and state expense (over $1 million between 1894 and 1904); unionism suffered a tremendous blow, and the state acquired a reputation for reactionism.

While news from the hard-rock districts was capturing newspaper attention, the same union-versus-owner friction was fomenting in the coal camps. Colorado had emerged by 1900 as one of the Rocky Mountain region's major coal producers, with the northern field (Boulder and Weld counties) and the southern field (Huerfano and Las Animas counties) leading the way. In contrast to its hard-rock cousin, coal mining was controlled by management with an iron hand. It dictated politics, told employees where to shop, and sneaked spies into the work force, none of which was characteristic of the hard-rock industry. Coal mining was more dangerous (319 miners died in accidents in 1910) and paid less; company towns appeared dreary and depressing.

Into the wretched lives of the miners (one reporter called them little removed from "downright slavery") came a ray of hope in the form of a union. The United Mine Workers moved in from the East and found exactly what it had endured at home — hostility, violence, blacklisting, and conflict. The coal mine owners fought with more unity and as much determination as their hard-rock counterparts in Telluride, Leadville, and Cripple Creek. Conflicts in 1901, 1903–04, and finally in 1913–14 led to the crisis in the southern field, which began in September 1913. The union called a strike, demanding a 10 percent wage increase, union recognition, and enforcement of Colorado mining laws, including the eight-hour day and health and safety regulations. Feisty eighty-two-year-old labor advocate and socialist Mary Harris "Mother Jones" rallied her "boys" to the cause. Both sides dug in, and the strike stretched into the winter.

Company guards and strikebreakers swarmed in; strikers escaped to tent colonies along the foothills. At last the National Guard, now a familiar oppressor of striking miners, advanced into the district. A confrontation was bound to occur; it came on April 20, 1914, at Ludlow Station, the site of the most prominent union tent colony. One side fired (both accused the other of firing the first shot), and before the shooting ended five miners and one trooper died, along with two women and eleven children who suffocated while huddling in a hole, desperately trying to avoid the fighting. The hatred was evident in a song entitled "Ludlow Massacre":

> That very night you soldiers waited
> Until us miners was asleep;
> You snuck around our little tent town,
> Soaked our tents with your kerosene.

Vengeful strikers overran the district before the army was finally sent in to quiet the disturbance. Congress and the national press investigated the Ludlow massacre, and the miners eventually gained better working conditions, shorter hours, and higher pay. The UMW, however, was driven out of the state, replaced by the so-called company unions.

Two decades of labor conflict ended that day; for better or worse, the new world was at hand. Once again nobody really won, everybody lost something, and national attention was focused on Colorado as it had not been since the boom days of Cripple Creek. The state attracted enough bad press to last a generation. Mining, too, would never be the same; its role as the primary ingredient of Colorado's economy had ended. A visitor's description of a declining and depressed Kokomo told more perhaps than the writer intended. A group of old people "slouched along the plank walls, with a far-away look in their eyes as if they had lost something which was never to come back to them." They had lost all hope; nothing beckoned them from over the next mountain.

As bad as the labor wars had been, Colorado's agony was not over. Politically, it emerged as one of the most reactionary of states. Major problems surfaced with the gubernatorial election of 1904 and its ludicrous aftermath, when the state had the questionable honor of having three governors in twenty-four hours. Charges of corruption, vote stealing, and graft permeated all levels of government. Durango's noted newspaper editor, David Day, threw up his hands in horror: "Unseating Alva Adams was a steal, an outrage, an assault upon human liberty and the ballot." The *Denver Post* blasted out that same March 1905, "The burning necessity of Colorado is taking a meat axe to the corporation tentacles that are thrust into every public affair."

What had caused these angry outbursts? They represented a reaction to a significant shift in society. Colorado, like all of America, was becoming urbanized and industrialized. The country was changing drastically from the agrarian-dominated society of the nineteenth century. Bryan's campaign of 1896 had been, in part, an attempt to stem the changing times, one that proved futile. Rural America lagged behind; the "yeoman farmer" no longer formed the backbone of the nation. Signs of the new times lay everywhere. Large corporations controlled the railroads, the coal mines, the smelters, and many of the major hard-rock mines. Denver, the largest city, was run by a political machine that would have compared well with the best of its genre in the East. In the towns and cities were found the best hospitals, libraries, theaters, and schools, as well as modern conveniences, varied businesses, stronger financial institutions, better-paying and more plentiful jobs, and an attractive lifestyle.

The downside of progress was exhibited by graft, corruption, intolerable working conditions, political machines, poverty, and slums. Colorado had two rotten political boroughs. The coal mining districts controlled by Republican companies (Colorado Fuel and Iron and Victor American Coal) and Robert Speer's Democratic machine in Denver could be counted on for devious political maneuvers.

The 1904 governor's race gave evidence of trouble that had been brewing for years. It pitted incumbent Republican James Peabody, the arch villain (from labor's point of view) in the crushing of the 1903–04 strikes, against Democrat Alva Adams. Fraud and irregular voting reached all-time highs. In the coal districts, voters were told that a Democratic victory would result in the closing of the mine and the loss of all jobs. To reinforce the point, management warned them that anyone who voted for Adams would be fired. Foreigners were naturalized in wholesale numbers before the election and told for whom to vote. The Speer machine matched the Republican tactics deed for deed, however. It actually sponsored schools to teach "repeaters" how to vote early and often. One Denver ward of 100 registered voters turned in 717 Democratic votes and 9 Republican ones; another had 134 voters with the same handwriting!

Adams's victory immediately prompted a Republican protest. The issue ended up on the legislative floor and before the court bench, both of which were controlled by the entrenched GOP, which had rebounded from the disaster of the 1890s. The legislative and judicial hearings disgraced Coloradans and their state as the dirty linen was aired for all to see. A strange compromise was eventually worked out: Adams resigned, to be replaced by Peabody for a day, and then by Lt. Governor Jesse McDonald.

Colorado was badly in need of reform to save itself from political chicanery and corporate control. Fortunately for Colorado, the United States was in the midst of what was known as the Progressive era. Wide-sweeping reforms were being instituted to clean up just such problems as the state faced. There were plenty of other problems in this first decade of the twentieth century: adulterated meats, white slave trade, stock market irregularities, fraudulent insurance companies, crime, slums, growing power and wealth in the hands of fewer people, and political scandals, to name just a few.

The heritage of the Populists lived on in the Progressive movement, although the latter was more urban, middle class and professionally oriented than the earlier agrarian- and miner-backed protest by the "have-nots." In Colorado the movement came to be symbolized by one of the finest governors ever to hold that office, John Shafroth, who served two terms, from 1909 to 1913. After resigning his congressional seat in 1904, when he discovered that he had won because of Speer-machine voting fraud, "Honest John" became a leader of the state reform movement. As governor, Shafroth had to fight the conservative Republicans and the Democratic Speer regulars in the legislature to succeed in passing his programs. A bitter battle ensued, which he lost during his first administration. Then, by taking his case to the people and the press and calling a special session of the legislature, he brought enough pressure to bear to win. As he told the legislators, "A shock to the moral sense, followed by a feeling of resentment, occurs when electors find that they have been duped and deceived."

Shafroth's sweeping reforms placed Colorado in the forefront of the Progressive movement. Initiative, referendum, and recall restored power to the "hands of the people." Besides these reforms, Colorado achieved a campaign expenses law, a tax commission, the regulation of children's and women's labor, the secret ballot, a state conservation commission, a stronger coal mine inspection law, home rule for cities and towns, a reorganized civil service commission, and one reform that was considered almost heretical by some: the recall of judicial decisions. This was popular government at its best. A man of principle, Shafroth singlehandedly helped to reverse the image of Colorado as one of the worst-governed states.

"Honest John" was loved by his supporters and hated by corporation/machine interests of both parties. Proving that he was indeed a twentieth-century man, Shafroth backed women's suffrage, good roads, and reclamation; as would any true westerner, he supported opening forest reserves to multiple use. Colorado was changing and he knew it, as these comments from his 1911 speech to the Good Roads Congress attest:

> It can not be a purely local question, but it is one where all receive a benefit, and that is solely from the commercial standpoint. When you consider that it is also important that these roads should be made good from the standpoint of pleasure, the standpoint of the automobilist, the effectiveness of the work and the results are apparent to everybody.

The Colorado to which he was referring needed better roads in part to handle the increasing tourist traffic. Tourism had always been a vital part of the state's economy; the railroads, Denver, and the hot springs dominated the industry for decades. Where railroads went, so did the tourist trade; only the most intrepid travelers preferred to venture beyond the tracks. Now, however, the automobile was making inroads and changing the nature of tourism. The state already had a national park, Mesa Verde, which was created in 1906 to preserve the ruins of Colorado's earliest inhabitants, the Anasazi. (A group of women, drawn from across the state and the nation, had championed that cause for a decade before Congress and President Theodore Roosevelt concurred with them.)

The state also harbored a bevy of national forests, over the ardent objections of many Coloradans who failed to realize the long-term benefits to be gained from conserving trees; they could see only that the old frontier tradition of utilizing all nearby natural resources for private gain had been severely restricted. Theodore Roosevelt, who loved the West and hunted in Colorado, championed the forests. The popular and dynamic T. R. always attracted a crowd; he found solitude by asking a Colorado Springs friend to pick a spot where he could have three days off "in rather wild country as it would discourage newspaper people from following us." No previous American president influenced the state as much as he did with parks, conservation, forests, and reclamation.

Conservation, a new idea for Coloradans, gained acceptance slowly, but Robert Speer saw to it that Denverites shared his image of "the city beautiful." This intriguing individual, both political boss and environmental dreamer, envisioned Denver as a city of grace and charm, an American Paris. To this end he improved the city's lighting, more than doubled the size of the city park and playground space, built the auditorium, planned the Civic Center, beautified Cherry Creek, improved the city zoo, encouraged the planting of trees, and started what became the Denver Mountain Parks system. The *Denver Post,* though often critical of him, ultimately lauded Speer's accomplishments after his death on May 14, 1918: "His vision was broad, his activities effective, forceful and unceasing. He was the creator of the 'City Beautiful.' "

In a sense, Speer and his Denver constituted Colorado at that time. Coloradans would be required to capture his vision in the upcoming years in order to protect everything they cherished about their state. Although Colorado still carried remnants from an earlier century, it was marching in step with the twentieth. The future promised to be as exciting as the past.

An 1896 presidential campaign parade for William McKinley at Tejon and Pike's Peak in Colorado Springs. The umbrellas were red, white, and blue with pictures of the candidate. The "Battle of the Standards," gold bugs versus silverites, captured Coloradans' political interest as did no other presidential election. *Courtesy Pikes Peak Library District, Colorado Springs.*

The second fire in Cripple Creek, April 1896. Cripple Creek gold helped pull the state out of the 1890s' depression. It was Colorado's last great gold rush and boom. *Courtesy Colorado College/Special Collections, Colorado Springs.*

The crash of 1893 was Colorado's worst to date. Unemployed workers flocked to Denver to find work. Work was not to be had, so some joined Jacob Coxey's army to march on Washington to demand government help. *Courtesy Denver Public Library/Western History Department.*

Coxey's "Navy yard" at 31st Street and the Platte River in Denver, June 6, 1894. The idea of floating downriver to the east quickly sank in the Platte. The depression lingered on for years, even as late as 1900 for some areas. *Photo by George Beam. Courtesy Colorado Historical Society, Denver.*

Cripple Creek, near Pike's Peak, exploded into the headlines in 1892–93. Its gold made millionaires and helped Colorado Springs grow as it hadn't for years. *Courtesy Colorado Springs Pioneers Museum.*

"Remember the Maine, to hell with Spain"; Colorado lightheartedly marched off to war in April 1898; by August it was all over. *Courtesy Carnegie Library, Boulder.*

The war's aftermath proved more painful than the actual event. "Our little brown brother" in the Philippines proved a tough opponent. Scouting party, Company C, of the First Colorado Infantry. *Courtesy Pueblo Library District.*

Camp McIntire of the Colorado National Guard, Leadville, 1896–97. From 1894 to 1914 labor violence rocked the state as unions and management squared off in coal and hard-rock districts. The Colorado National Guard repeatedly marched in, as it did at Leadville in 1896. The guard generally supported the owners. *Courtesy Pueblo Library District.*

Colorado National Guard on strike duty in Telluride, 1903–04, Lt. Lloyd Hill in front. The last two major mining districts, Cripple Creek and the San Juans, witnessed the final episodes of the labor wars in the hard-rock districts. When the smoke cleared, the unions were broken. *Courtesy Carnegie Library, Boulder.*

Cokedale was one of many company coal towns. The companies literally controlled the miners and their families from birth to grave. Colorado was one of the West's most important sources of coal. *Courtesy Aultman Museum, Trinidad.*

Hecla Heights, a Rocky Mountain Fuel Company coal town. This company town was built at Louisville in 1910 for strikebreakers and was well fenced for protection. Miners in the Louisville-Lafayette area began a strike in 1910 that lasted five years. Guards at the Hecla mine used searchlights and machine-gun fire to keep strikers away. *Courtesy Carnegie Library, Boulder.*

Mother Jones, the "most dangerous woman in America," marches in Trinidad during the 1913–14 labor conflict in the coal fields. The struggle came to a climax at Ludlow on April 20, 1914, when nineteen people were killed. Once again, Colorado's reputation was dragged through the mud. *Courtesy Colorado Historical Society, Denver.*

Funeral procession of Louis Tikas in Trinidad. United Mine Workers organizer and leader, Tikas was killed at Ludlow. Trinidad was in the heart of the southern coal field, one of Colorado's most significant. *Courtesy Colorado Historical Society, Denver.*

This sod house on the plains is reminiscent of "Little House on the Prairie." With the coming of dry-land farming methods, farmers returned to the plains in the early 1900s. Life was never easy, however, for either men or women. *Courtesy Pikes Peak Library District, Colorado Springs.*

The Shaw Brothers' homestead on Williams Fork near Craig, 1895. Isolated northwest Colorado was the last area of the state to be settled; its coal, oil, and oil shale booms were products of later decades. *Courtesy Museum of Northwest Colorado, Craig.*

The Wellington Wheel, Grand Junction area, ca. 1910. The wheel was used to lift water for irrigation, which promoters said would make the desert bloom. It did in some places, with adequate finances and hard work. *Photo by John Page. Courtesy Museum of Western Colorado, Grand Junction.*

Construction of the Gunnison Tunnel, looking upriver from the powerhouse. This was part of the Uncompahgre Reclamation Project, Colorado's first by the Bureau of Reclamation. The tunnel cost $2.9 million. *Courtesy Bureau of Reclamation, Denver.*

President William Howard Taft speaks at the opening of the Gunnison Tunnel. Construction began in 1904; Taft spoke in 1909, and the next year water from the Gunnison River reached the Uncompahgre Valley. It would be years before all the problems were worked out. *Courtesy Denver Public Library/Western History Department.*

Established in 1900, Swink (Otero County) opened with another plains farming excitement. Farm villages grew more slowly and less boisterously than mining settlements. *Courtesy Pueblo Library District.*

Ollie Beers, a Littleton high school student, irrigating, ca. 1907. Littleton and other Denver suburbs were rural settlements until the post-1945 boom. *Courtesy Littleton Historical Museum.*

Packing fruit at the Borum packing tent in Paonia, ca. 1910. Fruit was an important crop in the Grand Junction region and other Western Slope valleys almost from the time of initial settlement in the early 1880s. *Photo by W. S. Edwards. Courtesy Paonia Public Library.*

Germans from Russia work in the beet fields in the Greeley area. Colorado farmers hoped sugar beets would become their long-awaited cash crop. Sugar beets were first planted in 1893 near Grand Junction and were so successful they "migrated" to the Eastern Slope. The migration of Germans from Russia began in the nineteenth century, and by 1920 there were some 21,000 such immigrants in the state, particularly in northeastern counties. *Courtesy City of Greeley Museums.*

Horsepower in the wagon provided the power for threshing at the Horsley place at Livermore, near Fort Collins, ca. 1897. *Courtesy Fort Collins Public Library.*

Breaking the tough prairie sod to prepare for planting near Sterling, 1911. The settlement of much of eastern Colorado came after the turn of the century. *Courtesy Overland Trail Museum, Sterling.*

The Becker sisters branding cattle. In 1894 the sisters and their brother ran the family ranch in the San Luis Valley. Ranch women then and now did all of the jobs necessary to keep the operation going. *Photo by O. T. Davis. Courtesy Denver Public Library/Western History Department.*

Bertha Kaeperneck Blancett rides a bronc at Endicott in 1909. Raised in Atwood, Colorado, she was world champion woman rider in 1914–15. Women participated in many rodeo events in the early twentieth century. *Courtesy Overland Trail Museum, Sterling.*

Gateway, Colorado, ca. 1905. Gateway remains a small town on the west end of Unaweep Canyon in the Uncompahgre Plateau. It offers the state's longest growing season, over 200 days. *Courtesy Museum of Western Colorado, Grand Junction.*

Civil War veteran John Mobley was a lawman in Julesburg before moving to the Crystal Valley. He helped found Marble, ranched near Carbondale, and then moved to the Blue Mountains north of Rangely near the Utah border. He died in 1902. *Courtesy Rio Blanco Historical Society and White River Museum, Meeker.*

Main Street in Delta looking south, ca. 1893. Delta House is the first building on the right. Like most of the rest of the Western Slope, Delta was settled after the Ute removal. *Courtesy Delta County Historical Society, Delta.*

The famous Cherrelyn horse car that operated from Englewood to the Cherrelyn district at 4200 S. Broadway from 1892 to 1910. The horse pulled the car up the hill to Cherrelyn and then climbed on the rear platform and rode back down. *Courtesy Littleton Historical Museum.*

Vice president–elect Theodore Roosevelt "treed" by a bear cub in 1901. Roosevelt visited the Meeker area for a hunting trip with John Goff as his guide. *Courtesy Rio Blanco Historical Society and White River Museum, Meeker.*

The old and the new — horses and trucks — at 15th and Blake in Denver. Denver's population was 133,000 in 1900, thanks to an economic hinterland of mining and agriculture tied together by railroads. *Courtesy Tom Noel, Denver.*

Joe Wells, P. Fink, and Frank Nevill after a successful fishing trip on the Big Thompson. Nevill founded Sylvandale guest ranch at the mouth of Big Thompson Canyon. *Courtesy Loveland Museum and Gallery.*

Bert and Anna Mae Smith and a honeymoon tent at Green Mountain in the 1890s. *Photo by Wellington. Courtesy Ute Pass Historical Society, Woodland Park.*

A. Schmidt ski jumping at Hot Sulphur Springs in 1912. "Snowshoeing," as skiing was called, came with the miners in the 1860s. Within twenty years races were being held near Crested Butte, but the great development came after World War II. *Courtesy Grand County Museum, Hot Sulphur Springs.*

Ed Miles and Heck Litton tagging elk near Craig. Over the heated protests of many Coloradans, forest preserves, then national forests, were set aside in the 1890s and 1900s. Uncle Sam had come to stay, and his role would increase. *Courtesy Museum of Northwest Colorado, Craig.*

Baseball teams from Palisade and the Teller Institute, a Bureau of Indian Affairs school in Grand Junction, ca. 1902. Almost every town had its "nine," on whose victory or defeat rode local honor and bets. *Courtesy Museum of Western Colorado, Grand Junction.*

Bryan Cooper established a Christmas sleigh ride for children and a New Year's sleigh ride for adults in Craig. They were annual events for about a decade. The man in blackface acted as a servant to help people into the sleigh. *Photo by Dan W. Diamond. Courtesy Museum of Northwest Colorado, Craig.*

Marathon runners on Main Street, Littleton, April 16, 1909. The *Denver Post* marathon was from Littleton to the *Post* building at 15th and Champa in Denver. This event foreshadowed the jogging and running excitement of the 1970s and later. *Courtesy Littleton Historical Museum.*

The safety bike, second from right, eventually replaced these high wheelers. Coloradans of the 1890s went through the state's first bicycle craze. *Courtesy Denver Public Library/Western History Department.*

Patience Cairns Kemp playing in the snow at Grand Lake in 1911 at age twenty-three months. Kemp has been a historian of the Grand Lake area and remains active in 1991. *Courtesy Grand County Museum, Hot Sulphur Springs.*

"The Brass Band," the Del Norte school band, ca. 1916. Most schools in this period had a band that was the pride of the community. This San Luis Valley band is notable for its racial mix and for the efforts from that period to force cultural uniformity. In this particular case, at least one student had his name anglicized, apparently by the school administration. The student's last name was changed from Sierra to Mountain. *Courtesy Rio Grande County Museum, Del Norte.*

J. E. Winslow and Happy Jack out for a ride in Boulder in 1901. Children found a variety of entertainment available in these days before television and movies. *Photo by J. B. Sturtevant. Courtesy Carnegie Library, Boulder.*

William Johnson, Iva Melton, and Laura Bell, Pueblo-area pioneers. African-Americans faced discrimination throughout nineteenth-century Colorado. They were literally the "last hired and the first fired." *Courtesy Pueblo Library District.*

The fascination of tourists with glimpses of the "wild West" presented photographers with a growing market for their work. This photo of a Ute child and puppies was taken by W. R. Rowland sometime around World War I. *Courtesy La Plata County Historical Society, Durango.*

Max Stein was a Pueblo policeman and prominent Jewish businessman. Pueblo and other Colorado towns and cities, particularly Denver, Leadville, and Cripple Creek, had active Jewish communities. Hardly a town did not have a Jewish merchant. *Courtesy Pueblo Library District.*

Hispanic family and adobe home near Trinidad. Hispanics settled in the San Luis Valley and Trinidad area before 1859; later, they found the Anglo world to the north of them dominant and racist. *Courtesy Colorado Historical Society, Denver.*

Denver had the state's largest Chinese population and was the scene of a bitter anti-Chinese riot in 1880. This is Vee Wing's store in Colorado Springs, ca. 1902–12. *Courtesy Pikes Peak Library District, Colorado Springs.*

Dr. Ella Mead in her 1906 Maxwell. There had been women physicians in Colorado for a generation before Dr. Mead, but the profession remained nearly exclusively male. Mead drove this vehicle some 150,000 miles and did much of the maintenance on the car herself. In 1914 she established a system for recording vital statistics for Weld County. *Courtesy City of Greeley Museums.*

Denver, Cripple Creek, and Leadville had the most famous red-light districts. After 1900 Denver stood alone with its well-named Market Street, and the Club and its girls. *Courtesy Amon Carter Museum, Fort Worth, Texas.*

The Moffat Road in Denver. Colorado pioneer David Moffat's dream was to open the northwestern section of the state. He went bankrupt building a railroad over the Front Range, but others completed the project. *Photo by L. C. McClure. Courtesy Denver Public Library/Western History Department.*

Archie McLachlan's sawmill, twenty-five miles northeast of Craig. Lumbering came with the miners and was an important adjunct industry for mining. Mills were found throughout the mountains and valleys. *Courtesy Museum of Northwest Colorado, Craig.*

Drilling for oil in the Boulder vicinity began in the 1890s. Isaac Canfield, who previously had mined coal in the area, struck oil and gas in 1902. Soon nearly 100 oil companies were active in the region. Oil and gas were later discovered in other parts of the state, making important contributions to Colorado's economy throughout the twentieth century. *Courtesy Carnegie Library, Boulder.*

Stanley Steamers loaded with Loveland Current Events Club members prepare to start for Estes Park in 1911. The automobile provided a major stimulus to tourism in the twentieth century. Americans' love affair with their cars would change Colorado forever. *Courtesy Loveland Museum and Gallery.*

The Ramona Hotel in Cascade, ca. 1900. The railroads dominated tourism until the coming of the automobile. Hot springs were especially attractive to those suffering from a variety of aches and pains. *Photo by Wellington. Courtesy Ute Pass Historical Society, Woodland Park.*

First Antlers Hotel (center) in Colorado Springs, ca. 1890–96. William Jackson Palmer planned the town as a health resort and tourist community. Because of his British investors and their involvement, it was dubbed "Little London." *Courtesy Colorado Springs Pioneers Museum.*

Radcliff Hotel on Grand Mesa, 1894. In July 1901 a group of 100 men burned the hotel to the ground after a deputy game warden hired by William Radcliff shot a fisherman to prevent his fishing the Grand Mesa lakes. *Courtesy Delta County Historical Society, Delta.*

Camping near Hahn's Peak, ca. 1906. This woman not only handled the flapjacks, but she also was a fisherwoman and bird hunter. Hahn's Peak was the state's northernmost mining camp. *Courtesy Penrose Library, Colorado Springs.*

Girls' basketball team in Paonia. Most communities had girls' basketball, although it usually took a debate among parents, teachers, and the school board before such a "rash" activity was allowed. *Photo by W. S. Edwards. Courtesy Paonia Public Library.*

First Winter Carnival at Hot Sulphur Springs with John Peyer, Flora Brinker, Adeline Morgan, Mrs. Fuller, and Pansy Perry. Swiss-born Peyer started the first carnival at Maggie's Hill and helped give a boost to winter sports in Colorado. *Courtesy Grand County Museum, Hot Sulphur Springs.*

Colorow School, ca. 1895, in the Blue River Valley south of Kremmling. The group includes Maud, Nettie, and Tom Pharo, as well as Bill Yost. Thomas Pharo, father of the three children, was an emigrant from England who developed a major ranch on the lower Blue. *Courtesy Grand County Museum, Hot Sulphur Springs.*

The WCTU (Women's Christian Temperance Union) and a stern-looking Carrie Nation (far right) fought against "Demon Rum" and fallen women and men. The young people would face a variety of temptations despite Carrie's admonitions. *Courtesy Denver Public Library/Western History Department.*

III

A TIME TO BREAK DOWN, AND A TIME TO BUILD UP
1914–1941

CRESTED BUTTE'S *Elk Mountain Pilot* (August 6, 1914) devoted nearly one whole page to the outbreak of war in Europe. As in every coal mining community, the citizens of the town represented a cross-section of nationalities from eastern Europe; they were much more interested in the European situation than most Coloradans. In subsequent issues the editor continued to follow war developments, but attention quickly focused on the possibility that the war might improve the coal market.

Having read and heard about tensions in the Balkans or a crisis between Germany and England for so many years, Coloradans could not believe that war had really broken out. They probably agreed with an earlier article in the *Elk Mountain Pilot* on February 9, 1911, that proposed that the dropping of a "specially prepared handbomb from an aeroplane" made war so horrible a prospect that it "is likely to do much to promote peace." War had come to the world, and despite President Woodrow Wilson's admonition that Americans should be neutral in "thought, word and deed," they could not maintain that stance.

In these last years of peace before Coloradans sailed "over there," they lived a life quite different from that of their parents a generation before. Advertisements in the newspapers told the story:

Martinelli sings a delightful ballad of love and springtime. And on this new Victrola Record it will delight music-lovers the country over.

Announcing the opening of our new Powerine station on Speer Boulevard at Clarkson. Now it is possible to get our Powerine gas and AutoKrat Oil . . .

COOL! Cool comfort every ironing day — fretless, contented comfort — no wearying walking back and forth with an Electric Flat Iron.

In the big city the phonograph, electricity, indoor plumbing, automobiles, motion pictures, and even the aeroplane were irrevocably altering lifestyles. From Durango to Denver, trolley cars clanged up and down main streets, transforming former pedestrian communities into core centers with suburbs fanning out along the tracks.

Rural Colorado, though a step or two behind, still had reason to crow. The opening of the Gunnison Project in 1909 had brought cheers from the people of the Uncompahgre Valley. The *Montrose Press* expressed local sentiment well in its September 24, 1909, headlines: "First Water Turned Thru the Tunnel Yesterday by President Wm. H. Taft. Amid Cheering of Thousands Chief Executive Inaugurates Completion of Greatest Irrigation Project — Era of Prosperity for Uncompahgre Valley is Here." Although the valley did not quite metamorphose into the Garden of Eden, prosperity did come to Montrose, Delta, and their neighbors. Uncle Sam had run to the rescue of Colorado once again, as he had been doing since 1861. In the twentieth century, government projects involving water, national parks, and national forests (already in place) would constitute a prevailing theme.

Farther east, at an earlier irrigation project — the Union Colony and Greeley — so many of the original settlers were still alive in 1911 that the *Denver Post* felt compelled to claim that "Greeley people live longer than any other in the world." Whether they actually did mattered little except to locals. What did matter was that irrigation bolstered Colorado agriculture, which came to dominate the state's economy. The old mainstay, mining, faded in significance. Mineral production leveled off in Cripple Creek and the San Juans in the teens, then declined in the twenties. The older Leadville, Aspen, and Central City districts had long ago passed their prime, and throughout the state once-thriving communities neared, or attained, ghost-town status. St. Elmo, nestled in the mountains southwest of Buena Vista, showed all the signs of approaching its end. Town trustees resigned and moved away; the ones who remained skipped meetings, and a husband and wife (mayor and clerk) handled what little government was necessary. City appropriations dropped from over $2,000 in 1912 to less than $400 four years later. Victor had been larger and wealthier than St. Elmo, yet even here the council had to notify Denver's Children's Hospital that "owing to financial conditions" the city could not "at this time make a donation." To economize further council members abolished the position of water collector, and at a June 1913 special meeting, called because a "financial emergency exists," they borrowed $2,000 from the Bank of Victor to meet expenses.

Tourists were attracted to these relics of the past, hoping to find traces of a dying, exciting era before they disappeared forever. Colorado native and future poet laureate Thomas Hornsby Ferril caught the scene beautifully in a poem he entitled "Ghost Town":

> Here's where the conifers long ago
> When there were conifers cried to the lovers;
>   Dig in the earth for gold while you are young!
> Here's where they cut the conifers and ribbed
> The mines with conifers that sang no more,
> And here they dug the gold and went away,
> Here are the empty houses, hollow mountains,
> Even the rats the beetles and the cattle
> That used these houses after they were gone
> Are gone; the gold is gone,
> There's nothing here,
> Only the deep mines crying to be filled.

Coloradans were generally too busy escaping that part of their history to notice that it was vanishing. In a sense, they were creating a past the way they imagined it, based on a romantic concept of that earlier era. Dime novels and Wild West shows fed their imaginations. Eventually they would come to embrace their real past, profit from it, and appreciate the heritage it gave to them.

Tourists were also beginning to invade the state's two national parks, especially Rocky Mountain National Park, created in 1915. Enos Mills and others had long advocated preservation of this beautiful alpine region, and it instantly became one of Colorado's most popular attractions. It was, as Estes Park people were fond of saying, "only three hours" by automobile from Denver; by 1919 just under 170,000 visitors had flocked to it, a number that exceeded the combined visitor totals of Yellowstone, Yosemite, Glacier, and Sequoia national parks. The statistics provided irrefutable evidence of the state's attraction and the importance of Denver as a tourist destination. By contrast, Mesa Verde graphically testified to the disadvantages of being located in an isolated corner of Colorado. Not until a dirt road was completed over Wolf Creek Pass did the visitor total top 1,000 (in 1916), and it took another ten years for it to surpass 10,000. Governor Shafroth and others who pushed for good roads were right on the mark. The *Mancos Times-Tribune* expressed the idea succinctly: "With good highways connecting with the east and west, Southwest Colorado would soon become one of the favorite haunts of the summer tourists in America" (August 24, 1917). To try to reach that end, towns and merchants joined the Santa Fe Trail Association, the Spanish Trails Association, and similar organizations that promoted "good roads" and their members' interests.

The automobile clearly was making an impact on Colorado, even though most Coloradans did not yet own one. The first car did not chug into Mesa Verde until 1914, but when it did Uncle Sam already had regulations in place. Fees of $1 for a single trip or $5 for the season were demanded upon arrival, and an eight-miles-per-hour speed limit in "straight stretches" was enforced. If no horses came into view, the speed could be increased to fifteen miles per hour. If a team was coming, the autos were required to pull to the "outer edge of the roadway," stop their motors, and "remain at rest until the team passed." For a few more moments in history "Old Dobbin" still commanded the right-of-way.

Coloradans were also keeping a wary eye on Europe as the war dragged into its second, and then its third, year, and they were bombarded with propaganda, particularly by the British and their allies. Hostilities were already having an impact on the state. The agricultural economy benefited and would continue to do so into 1919; English and European markets opened as seldom before. The amount of acreage planted in wheat tripled to over 1.3 million acres. Mining, too, cashed in briefly; the base metals — lead, zinc, copper — were needed for war manufacturing and rose in price. A sharp increase in the use of tungsten, used to harden steel, brought a small boom to the Nederland area, complete with "auto stages" and motion picture theaters. Vanadium, mined in the Paradox Valley, prospered as well, because it was a component of steel manufacturing. On the other hand, the war closed the European uranium market, which had been the major reason for prospecting and operating small mines near Newmire and Placerville, west of Telluride.

After three years of observing and becoming more and more involved emotionally, the United States entered the conflict in April 1917 — the "war to end all wars," it would be called, and the war to "make the world safe for democracy." The *Weekly Durango Democrat* of April 13 proudly noted that a flag had been planted on Smelter Mountain above town: "Our flag floats high above our heads, sending a message that Durango and its environs are Americans all, Americans all and forever." Coloradans pulled together for an all-out effort to win the war and busied themselves in patriotic endeavors. The governor established a council for defense, and the legislature, in a special session, appropriated emergency funds for the war effort. When the Colorado National Guard was federalized, one of its first duties was to guard the state's industrial and agricultural facilities. Some 43,000 men volunteered for, or were drafted into, the armed services, 326 of whom would die in battle. Coloradans supported their "Sammies" with send-off rallies and gifts after they settled in camp.

The main impact of World War I, however, came on the home front. Coloradans bought war bonds in Victory and Liberty drives, paid increased taxes, grew war gardens in vacant lots, organized Red Cross work, attended patriotic rallies, saved materials needed for the war, listened to talks by the "four-minute men" at their movie theaters, and cheerfully complied with the home front campaigns for meatless, wheatless, lightless, or gasless days or nights. Old and young cooperated in the war effort and tracked the war's progress in the newspapers. By June 1918, 11,000 boys and girls from areas outside Denver had enrolled in agricultural and garden clubs under trained supervision.

The "Great Crusade" brought out the best in Coloradans — and also the worst. Americans learned to hate the "Hun" and discovered that hate is an emotion difficult to turn off. The *Elk Mountain Pilot* advised its readers of foreign birth that they did not "need to fear any invasion of their personal or property rights" (April 26, 1917); no such assurances were given to German-Americans. Coloradans feared spies, sabotage, and the infiltration of German agents into their state, to the point of cautioning that householders should scrupulously avoid salespeople with Teutonic accents. Some local citizens searched for spies, reported their neighbors' suspected subversive activities and tried to root out all evidence of German culture and influence. These zealots burned books by German authors, pressured school boards to quit teaching German in the schools, worried that German words were corrupting English, feared that German music would stimulate all the wrong passions, and watched any neighboring German-Americans with a suspicious eye. Verbal and sometimes physical attacks descended upon persons who deviated even slightly from the patriotic line. Hate would be one of the legacies of the war into the 1920s.

The war lasted for only nineteen months, ending on November 11, 1918. Montrose celebrated with "scores of autos loaded with citizens" racing up and down Main Street as the riders shot guns and "anything that would explode." Whistles, sirens, auto horns, and the fire bell "kept up a merry warfare noise for about three hours." Hundreds of shots riddled the dummy of the Kaiser that hung on a corner. For Coloradans, the war had been too easy, too quick; the full impact of what had happened since 1914 had not sunk into their minds and lives.

They hardly had time to adjust to the changes before an even greater threat engulfed them, the flu epidemic of 1918–19. This worldwide disaster struck the high mountain valleys particularly hard; Silverton, population 1,150, reported 833 influenza and 415 pneumonia cases, with 146 deaths. A person could be well in the morning and dead by evening. Nurse Bessie Finegan remembered, "There was nobody on the streets [of Durango] that didn't have to go. Everybody wearing masks. I was no sicker than the rest but I couldn't walk I was so weak . . . Two things happened to you. Suddenly you couldn't breathe, or else you hemorrhaged." Masks, quarantines, a prohibition against public meetings, school closures, limited meat-eating, patent medicines — nothing stopped, or even slowed, the infectious plague. In early 1919 the epidemic began to wane, but in over ten months 7,783 Coloradans had died, a shocking total. Lesser outbreaks in following years never approached the enormity of this one. Coloradans, like all Americans, tried to forget it, but not even the Roaring Twenties could erase the horror from this generation's memory.

The war ended, the flu epidemic receded, and Coloradans turned their attention to their new world. Reform had gone the way of all good things, as Americans tired of trying to improve themselves — they wanted to relax. They sought to return to "normalcy," a word popularized later by Warren Harding. That would be difficult to accomplish, no matter how hard they tried. The agricultural boom busted in 1919–20, and the farmer and rancher would suffer during the next decade; declining prices, debt burdens, surpluses, and isolation from the mainstream of American life set them adrift in a world that underappreciated their efforts. Tungsten, uranium, and molybdenum production collapsed in the postwar era, victims of less demand and foreign competition. Mining, however, was far from the minds of Coloradans as they moved into the new decade.

The war's legacy of hate and distrust was not so easily shed. It overshadowed the state and influenced individual lives for a decade. A nationwide resurgence of nationalism, which stressed the virtues of Americanism, contributed more tinder to an already volatile mix. The first sign of trouble came with the Red Scare; communism seemed to be on the march, and Americans feared this foreign ideology. The scare created several years of turmoil during which the Colorado legislature passed a law prohibiting the display of the "red flag" in public. Suspected radicals were rounded up, and a violent 1920 Denver Tramway strike was blamed on "reds." The *Denver Post* spotlighted statements such as this: "If you don't want the majority to rule, then go back to Russia"

(January 1, 1920). The shrill voices of suspicion and hatred finally receded before reemerging in a different form.

Many of the same forces at work during the red hysteria brought the Ku Klux Klan into power in mid-decade. This anti-foreign, anti-Catholic, anti-Semitic group opposed anyone or anything that displayed even mildly anti-American attitudes. The KKK fit right in with the climate of the era. The Klan had been gaining power nationally when it suddenly achieved outstanding success in Colorado. Wrapping itself in patriotism, morality, and middle-class virtues, the Klan projected an image of being just another popular service club, and many Coloradans fell for such an appeal. Political successes in Denver eventually translated into statewide control of the Republican party, which elected Clarence Morley as governor in 1924. From Julesburg to Grand Junction, and from Bayfield to Pueblo, the Klan marched and burned its crosses; in rural and urban Colorado it held sway. People from all walks of life participated in its parades and partook of its ritualistic mumbo jumbo. Durango's Rich McComb remembered what it did to his community: "It just created enemies, really. It was bad. It was pretty active here and it didn't do the town a damn bit of good."

Then, as quickly as it rose to power, the Klan declined in 1925–26. Opposition to the group intensified, and some newspapers continued to bombard it with ridicule. Politicians of both parties stood up against it. Adherents fell away when the Klan's state and national leaders failed to live up to the high goals it had set. Coloradans at last came to their collective senses, realizing just what this organization stood for and what it planned to do. The entire Klan episode remains to this day an ugly blot on the history of Colorado.

Another contributing factor to the rise of the Klan lay in the rapid changes that overtook the nation and the state during the twenties. Fearful of today and tomorrow, insecure people longed for what seemed to be simpler times, the good old days of yesteryear. Some differences were mere social manifestations of the new era — women smoking in public, opposition to Prohibition, new morals among youth and the "in" crowd, and the impact of the automobile. Other changes were more profound and fearsome, namely the disarrayed condition of Colorado's mining and agriculture and the declining importance of rural America.

Colorado and its residents were greatly altered by the "great war" and the decade following it. One new institution, Prohibition, was envisioned as the ultimate reform but actually led to lawlessness when many Coloradans winked at sneaking into the local speakeasy for a drink. During the 1920s, no year saw fewer than 500 arrests in the state for violating Prohibition, and on two occasions the total exceeded 1,000. Just as Klan activity mirrored postwar social unrest, so did the local response to national Prohibition. Old mining towns like Leadville and Silverton found new sources of income as havens for bootlegging. The controversy split a church congregation in Holyoke when the Sunday school superintendent was found imbibing. It created gang wars between Denver and Pueblo outlaws and incited Bayfield's Klan to hunt down local bootleggers (the KKK upheld Prohibition). Coloradans eventually agreed that the "noble experiment" had failed, and in 1933 both state and national Prohibition ended.

Other Coloradans were greatly distressed by Hollywood's morals and movies. Such advertising slogans as "Petting Parties in the Purple Dawn" threatened to degrade morals and subvert gullible youth. The Charleston, blackbottom, and other dances also undermined standards, as did the flapper dress and the continuing allurement of the bright lights of the city. Some men blamed the whole debacle on giving women the right to vote!

The social changes brought on by the automobile generated further anxiety for many people. The new freedom from traditional social restraints — changes in courting practices, Sunday drives that hurt church attendance, and youths cruising the main drag — fueled fears. But other Coloradans became enamored of the automobile in the 1920s. At $290 for a Ford, the car was more than just a dream for most of them. It alleviated the isolation of farm and ranch, broadened the tourist base, inspired new businesses, and stimulated the Colorado oil industry (Boulder/Fort Collins field), including oil shale for a brief time. Denver's *Oil Shale Outlook* promised "this paper is boosting what will be the greatest industry west of the Mississippi within ten years" (April 20, 1921). De Beque and other nearby towns held out high hopes, but, alas, the boom had busted by the mid-twenties. Oil shale may have failed, but Colorado's oil production grew along with that of Texas and Oklahoma. Not everyone was impressed, though. The president of the Colorado School of Mines issued a warning in 1921: "The average middle-aged man of today will live to see the virtual exhaustion of the world's supply of oil from wells."

The tourist industry was one of the larger beneficiaries of the automobile. Denver, still the most common destination point for travelers, opened Overland Park along the banks of the South Platte for the "motor gypsies." One pleased camper said in 1924, "We were impressed with Colorado, which had better roads than other states because Colorado used a gas tax to improve them. Denver's Overland Park was one of the finest we struck on all our cross country trips." However, among the auto's negative impacts were the continued decline of railroads, the ending of careers for blacksmiths and livery stable operators, and the threat of altered business patterns on main streets.

Transportation was changing in another way — the airplane was evolving from a barnstorming attraction into a practical solution to Colorado's geographic isolation. Denver again seized the initiative and opened the state's first municipal airport in 1919; within two years 3,600 passengers were utilizing its services. Air service was augmented a few years later by cargo planes that flew to Denver, Colorado Springs, and Pueblo.

Perhaps the most important development of the decade over the long run was the introduction of regional water compacts, or, as they are popularly known, "treaties." Colorado, which had pioneered in the evolution of water law — "first in time, first in right," combined with beneficial use — now found itself in the vanguard of a new approach to regulation of water resources. Most of the major rivers of the region originate in Colorado, which created entanglements with neighbors who wanted a share of the water flowing out of the mountains. The most important discussions dealt with the Colorado River.

The Colorado River and its tributaries flow through seven western states, which are divided by the Grand Canyon into the upper basin (Colorado, Wyoming, Utah, New Mexico) and the lower basin (Arizona, California, Nevada). All rely in some manner on the river for water. Coloradans believed their claims held priority because the Colorado Rockies gave birth to the stream. The states first convened in 1919 to explore their common problems; subsequent meetings brought in a new participant, the United States government. Federal, state, and local interests needed definition and protection. As a result, in 1922 the Colorado River Compact was negotiated, a milestone in water development. Another seven years passed before all the states and the federal government ratified the compact (Arizona actually refused, only to see Congress rule that six out of seven would suffice), and it was declared in force. Water in the amount of 7.5 million acre-feet was guaranteed each year to both basins, out of what was assumed to be an average of 20 million acre-feet of annual flow. The whole issue proved to be far from resolved, however, as the next generations of westerners would discover.

Achieving a balanced distribution of water among the states proved to be easier than achieving balanced economic growth in Colorado. If the Roaring Twenties actually roared, they did it in the cities, where most of the modern conveniences could be found, jobs were more plentiful, and life for middle-class Americans appeared more prosperous than it did for their rural and small-town cousins. On the farms, in the mining communities, and at the coal mines, times were tough. The railroads' dwindling use of coal, combined with the introduction of natural gas, drastically cut the demand for coal for industrial and domestic purposes. Agriculture continued its economic slide, which started after the war, and there seemed no way out of the depression for farmers or farm villages. An economic downturn of equal magnitude engulfed the mining districts — gold, silver, and lead production all remained suppressed, and zinc, copper, and molybdenum mines nearly suspended operations. Smelters closed, communities declined, county tax bases collapsed; mining fell into the doldrums.

Even Colorado's urban economy was hardly as prosperous as it might have looked at a quick glance; in truth, it had encountered serious trouble by 1929. That year, when the "end of the poorhouse was in sight" according to President Herbert Hoover, turned out instead to be the one that nearly put most Americans *into* the poorhouse. The stock market crash of October triggered the events that plunged the country into the Great Depression. It battered almost all Coloradans over the next twelve months and seemed to worsen with the passage of each year as the 1930s moved dismally along. The Boulder *Daily Camera*, trying to keep up appearances, nevertheless reported on October 1, 1930, "Even in prosperous Boulder more money to provide for families of the unemployed is asked for — seems to be needed."

Statistics tell the grim tale. Colorado Fuel and Iron, the Denver & Rio Grande Railroad, and a host of other companies went into receivership. Department store sales fell by almost 33 percent, and more than 25 percent of Coloradans found themselves out of work. Nearly a third of the banks in the state closed their doors, and Denver itself faced bankruptcy by the end of 1933. Farm prices dropped to record lows; swamped relief agencies ran out of money.

To make matters worse in eastern Colorado, nature played a cruel card, dealing out drought and wind. The infamous dust storms of the early thirties made midday seem like night in Holly and Burlington. Dust blocked roads, suffocated livestock and poultry, made breathing difficult, ruined crops, and dried up hopes. Baca, Las Animas, and Prowers counties were especially hard hit, unable to raise much of anything during the worst four years. Farmers abandoned the land, as they had previously; the exodus carried many of them right into the cities, where problems were already acute.

The real story of the Depression is found in the lives of people. Denver's Reverend Edgar Wahlberg recalled, "Among the dark shadows of the Depression years were the haunted jungles of homeless men." His church tried to help with food, meals, and other things. "In those days, dog food was pure horsemeat

... The grocery stores found it hard to keep up with demand." One grocery was convinced that there were a lot of dogs in Wahlberg's neighborhood, to which he replied that "for the time being it was human food." A Durango woman told of losing her home: "We couldn't make the taxes . . . so we just walked out, didn't get a dime out of it." A resident of Rockville, a little coal camp outside Florence, remembered: "Times were rough. You could buy pork chops in Florence for ten cents a pound but nobody could buy them 'cause they didn't have a dime." One young man was never able to attend college because the money saved for his education was lost when an insurance company failed. Historian David Lavender recalled the desolation at Ouray, where he went looking for work at the Camp Bird Mine:

> On a bitter cold January day I landed in Ouray. It was a gloomy little town, with down-at-the-heel brick buildings lining the main street, an astonishing rococo hotel, and rows of widely spaced, once-handsome frame houses radiating out from the remnants of the business district. Over it all hung the ineffable sadness of departed wealth.

Mining wealth had long ago departed Ouray; now the depression settled over the spectacular site and across the state. Happy days were decidedly not here again, despite the picture portrayed by the hit tune of the era. Coloradans and most Americans were more than ready for a change in circumstances by 1932. Out went Hoover and the Republicans, in came Franklin Roosevelt and his vaguely described New Deal. Republicans feared what that "wild Democrat" would do when he moved into the White House. Within days they found out. The initial impact came from the national bank holiday; during the next six years the New Deal would bring as much change to Colorado as the twenties had.

The 1932 election also brought rustic, conservative Democrat Edwin "Big Ed" Johnson to the governor's chair. Johnson did not embrace most of the New Deal and fought it with varying success during his two terms. Part of his ambivalence arose from the state's long-term love-hate relationship with the federal government and the fear of too much federal control. Johnson was especially unhappy when the state was pressured into providing matching funds for some of Uncle Sam's projects. Over his objections, and with a great deal of posturing, Colorado received approximately $396 million in federal relief and recovery funds.

When New Dealers and others tried to unseat Johnson in 1934, they selected progressive coal mine owner and social worker Josephine Roche, one of Colorado's outstanding twentieth-century women, to run against him. However, Johnson had enough political clout and savvy to withstand the challenge and went on to be elected senator two years later.

New Deal money came to Colorado from a variety of agencies, the famous "scrambled alphabet," as Washington rushed to provide relief, recovery, and finally reform. One of the earliest and most popular programs was the Civilian Conservation Corps (CCC), which put unemployed young men to work while providing for their medical, dental, and educational needs. Each participant signed up for a six-month tour of duty, lived in the camps under the direction of army officers, and sent $25 of his $30 monthly salary home. The work varied; CCC boys built dioramas for Mesa Verde, constructed Red Rocks Park near Denver, cleaned up Boulder's Flagstaff Mountain Park, built roads and bridges, improved national forests and lands, and fought forest fires. More than 30,000 men had passed through the Colorado camps before they closed in 1942. Both the young men and the state benefited from this program. Summarizing his CCC experiences, Coyne Thompson spoke for many: "It was a growing-up education. By the time you left, you were able to cope with the world at large. It was a good experience, there wasn't any doubt about it."

The Works Progress Administration was equally active within the state, employing at one time 43,000 Coloradans. The WPA improved or constructed 9,000 miles of state highways, built sewage plants, modernized waterworks, and built hundreds of public structures — a library at Greeley, a swimming pool for Fort Morgan, and a town hall at Center, for example. It hired people from all walks of life, unskilled to professional. Women were employed to make clothing, prepare schools, and run nurseries. Researchers conducted interviews, gathered historical data, and compiled a state guidebook, *Colorado: A Guide to the Highest State*. Artists painted murals, weavers repaired old textiles, actors and actresses performed, and a federally financed symphony orchestra gave concerts.

There were objections, of course, to these programs. Complaints of wasted funds, government bureaucracy, and "boondoggling" by workers surfaced almost as soon as the projects got started. Jim Sartoris explained that many of the men leaning on rakes or sitting down did not have the physical stamina to work a full day because of malnutrition. "There was a lot of criticism. I know they used to ridicule people about WPA this and WPA that, but, believe me, it had its good points. Because they worked for what they got."

A host of other projects was planned or underwritten by the New Deal, including gold-panning classes on the South Platte River in Denver. Panning even a fraction of an ounce of gold (raised to $35 by FDR) was more than most unemployed could hope to make elsewhere. So back went the hopeful to Gilpin, Clear Creek, and Boulder counties to pan the streams again where it had all begun. The wheel had come full circle since 1859.

The most ingenious and gigantic of all the federal projects, however, was the Colorado–Big Thompson, designed to bring Western Slope water to the Big Thompson and South Platte valleys. The idea had been percolating for years, but until the 1930s it had never come near to being realized. Even then, compromise and skillful diplomacy were required to bring all groups together to present a united front. Western Slopers worried about losing their water, particularly in dry years; they demanded, and finally received, storage reservoirs. Congress approved them, and President Roosevelt signed the bill in late 1937. The massive project would not be completed until the 1950s, although the first water flowed through the Alva B. Adams Tunnel to Eastern Slope farms in 1947. By the time of completion it included power plants, canals, ten reservoirs, fifteen dams, and twenty-four tunnels, at a cost of $164 million, nearly four times the original estimate.

The New Deal touched all Coloradans, from Main Street merchants to miners in the mountains. The $35-an-ounce gold price bestirred miners, as well as panners, and mining activity was resumed. Merchants encountered new regulations they must abide by, which arose from efforts to raise wages, shorten working hours, and increase employment. Because the state was slowly pulling out of the Depression, merchants objected to the restrictions. Labor unions profited when the Wagner Act of 1935 legalized collective bargaining. Agriculture also got some relief from the New Deal planners, who tried to bring order out of a chaotic situation. The Agricultural Adjustment Act (1933) paid the farmer for curtailing production of crops and animals. Soil conservation programs, new farming techniques, experimental seeds, and tree-planting campaigns were encouraged. The Taylor Grazing Act, passed in 1934, withdrew land and organized grazing districts to regulate the use and stop the abuse of public lands. In an extreme measure, farmers from "dusted" eastern counties were resettled in the San Luis Valley and elsewhere on the Western Slope to remove their "submarginal" farmland from production.

The Taylor Grazing Act would prove especially important over the years. Hayden lawyer and rancher Farrington Carpenter quickly saw its significance:

"I felt that it constituted one of the most important advances in the entire history of the public domain. It was the first attempt by Congress to add grass to the list of those natural resources that should be conserved and whose productivity should be improved." Although a lifelong Republican, Carpenter was appointed director of the grazing division and turned the act's words into deeds (his achievements included writing a federal range code) despite some heated objections from disgruntled ranchers, who saw only government regulation and loss of their rights.

The New Deal had come to Colorado and, in many ways, conquered it. Colorado ranked tenth among the forty-eight states in per capita expenditures by selected New Deal agencies during the period 1933–39. Just as opponents had feared, it was now to Washington, rather than to Denver, that many turned for help. Power lost by the state had been picked up by the federal government. There were Coloradans who feared just this kind of centralization and loss of local control; to them the New Deal was anathema. Yet there were others who enthusiastically supported the national policies of Roosevelt; they found his programs an invasion of privacy that they could live with.

Boosters of Colorado were not embarrassed when the Denver Chamber of Commerce boasted that the city had more government offices than any other city except Washington, D.C., nor were they unhappy to hear Denver referred to as the "second capital." On the other hand, some took pride in Ed Johnson's rebelliousness and that of some other politicians as well. It seemed to reinforce their own cherished notions of western independence. Some Durango businessmen, for example, could rail against the New Deal while watching their own economic prospects improve; at the same time, they lobbied the government to convert the abandoned smelter into some kind of federal project or to reopen it as a factory.

The trauma of these two decades became evident in Colorado's population growth — not since the 1860s had it been so small. The 1.1 million Coloradans of 1940 represented a gain of fewer than 200,000 in twenty years. The percentage of foreign-born had sunk steadily since 1910, reflecting the changing state economy.

The 1930s may have been depressed, but Coloradans could still plan for the future. Central City was long past its glory days when the idea for an opera festival was proposed. It came to fruition in 1932 in the restored opera house and has since emerged as one of the nation's most successful festivals. Aspen, too, declined to a mere shell of its former glory, yet some visionaries saw dollar signs buried in the snow that had so bedeviled mining and transportation. On

November 19, 1936, the *Aspen Times* headlined a featured article, "Winter Resort Plans are Revealed; Aspen May become Leading Snow Sports City in Entire United States." It seemed an impossible dream then, but no more impossible than what had been envisioned for Colorado many years earlier.

But while Coloradans looked ahead, the world situation deteriorated, a trend that would postpone Aspen's rise as the nation's ski capital. The world-wide depression had created a volatile international situation, out of which ambitious dictators arose with aspirations of empires of their own. By mid-decade it was almost too late to reverse the drift toward war. When it came in September 1939, knowledgeable Americans were not surprised; the only question was when the United States would enter it. Within a year the country was placing itself on a war footing; the humming military-industrial economy finally pulled the country out of the Depression. Colorado had reached another turning point in its history, but as yet Coloradans were unaware of it. Never before in its history had the state lived through two such crucial decades as the ones just passed.

Prominent politicians Casimiro Barela and William "Billy" Adams. Barela, from Trinidad, served in the Colorado legislature from 1871 to 1912. Adams, from Alamosa, was governor from 1927 to 1933 and strongly opposed the Klan. *Courtesy Adams State College, Alamosa.*

Europe went to war in 1914, America in 1917. After listening to three years of war horrors and British propaganda, Americans (including these Montrose volunteers) rushed to the colors "to make the world safe for democracy." *Courtesy Montrose County Historical Society Museum, Montrose.*

Colleges and universities went to war. World War I SATC radio school on the Colorado College campus. *Courtesy Colorado College/Special Collections, Colorado Springs.*

World War I was over relatively quickly, and citizens throughout the state celebrated Armistice Day. Denver, 16th and Tremont, November 11, 1918. *Courtesy Denver Public Library/Western History Department.*

Buying Liberty and Victory bonds was the patriotic thing to do. The tank, submarine, and plane were three military innovations during the war. This tank attempted to climb Pike's Peak during a 1919 bond promotion; here it is being christened "Little Zeb" with water. *Courtesy Pikes Peak Library District, Colorado Springs.*

A gathering of the Ku Klux Klan in the 1920s. Klan members were prominent members in many communities. Baptist minister Fred Arnold of Cañon City was Exalted Cyclops, and the Klan captured the Republican party and elected Clarence Morley governor in 1924. Within two years, the Klan's power collapsed, scandals wrecked the organization, and Coloradans came to their senses. *Courtesy Tom Noel, Denver.*

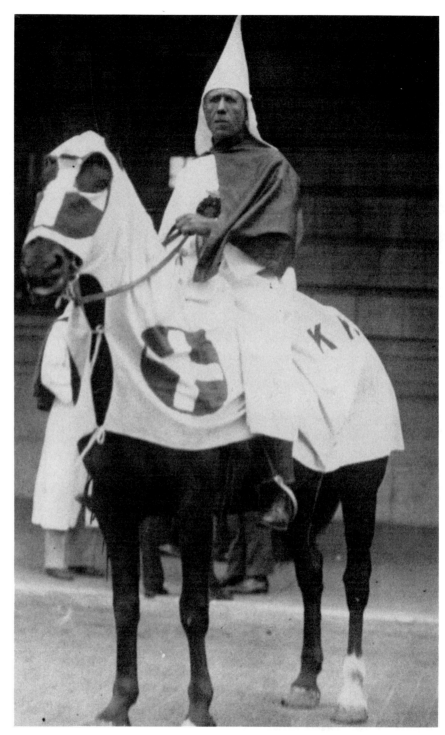

Reuben Hershey of the Ku Klux Klan in Denver, 1926. Hershey was a Denver city official under Mayor Benjamin Stapleton. The Klan rose to power in 1924–25 across all parts of the state. *Courtesy Colorado Historical Society, Denver.*

Prohibition agents "capture" a still in northeastern Colorado. Bootlegging occurred in small town and large city alike. *Courtesy Fort Morgan Museum.*

This photograph of a Japanese school in Swink in the 1920s illustrates Colorado's ethnic diversity. The number of Japanese-Americans living in the state was never great; many worked as farmers. *Courtesy Pueblo Library District.*

Black social clubs and churches were only a couple of indications of de facto segregation in the cities. Colorado was not alone; this tragedy was all too common throughout the country. *Courtesy Pueblo Library District.*

Harry Hoffman's in the 1930s. Hoffman, a member of Denver's Jewish community, owned a famous discount liquor store for decades. *Courtesy Rocky Mountain Jewish Historical Society, Denver.*

Bonny Bryant's Band was popular during the 1930s. By the time of the Depression, most blacks lived in cities. *Courtesy Pueblo Library District.*

Dearfield, a black colony near Greeley, was founded by O. T. Jackson, who purchased the land. At its 1921 peak, 700 people were in the colony, but sagging farm prices and the Depression sealed its doom. By the early 1930s, most residents had returned to the cities. *Courtesy City of Greeley Museums.*

Threshing machine in Craig, 1920 — steam tractor, thresher, and trailer. Farming, which boomed during the war, had already slipped into the doldrums. When the crash came in 1929, farmers had known hard times for a decade. *Photo by George Welch. Courtesy Museum of Northwest Colorado, Craig.*

H. R. Koepsel drives a plow in Kiowa County southeast of Eads, April 15, 1936. The tractor never replaced the horse on some farms and ranches. *Courtesy Colorado State University/Photographic Archives, Fort Collins.*

Reese and Charlie Tucker of Glenwood Springs (ages eleven and nine, respectively) spent the summer by themselves at a Tucker sheep camp near New Castle in 1918. The boys assumed this responsibility because labor was in short supply during the war. *Photo by Tucker. Courtesy Fort Lewis College/Center of Southwest Studies, Durango.*

Sheep on Ophir Pass in southwest Colorado, 1939. The Rio Grande Southern ran near here, and cattle and sheep were important "passengers." Trucks killed the railroad's business, and the number of sheep raised in Colorado declined steadily after mid-century as Americans' eating habits and clothing styles changed. *Courtesy Colorado State University/Photographic Archives, Fort Collins.*

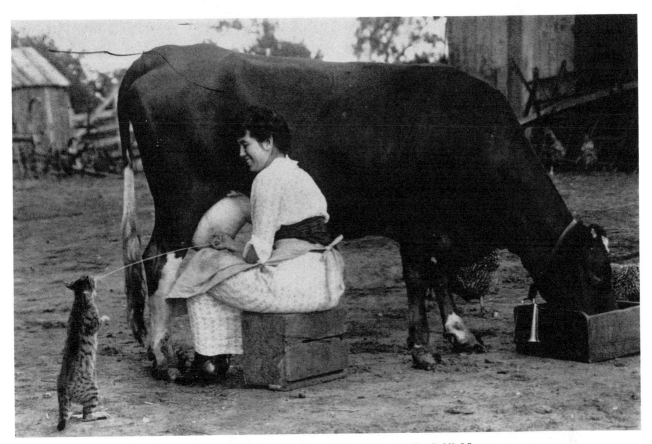
A moment of pleasure for a farm wife during a long day of hard work. *Courtesy Fort Collins Public Library.*

Women engineering students at the University of Colorado, ca. 1935; Professor Margaret Read teaches the technical drawing class. College women were finding more professional opportunities open to them. *Courtesy University of Colorado/Western Historical Collections, Boulder.*

In 1928 the WCTU was still trying to save America. Prohibition was not working, much to the horror of these determined ladies. "Dry" Herbert Hoover was running against "wet" Al Smith. *Courtesy Denver Public Library/Western History Department.*

Americans of the 1920s became quite sports minded. Big-time college football, boxing, baseball, tennis, and golf were most popular. Colorado Springs women practice putting in 1915. *Courtesy Colorado Springs Pioneers Museum.*

All-girl bands were novelties in the 1920s; here, Billie Stein's band strikes a pose for the photographer. Some Americans thought the country would not survive jazz and the Charleston. *Courtesy Rocky Mountain Jewish Historical Society, Denver.*

Josephine Roche, president of Rocky Mountain Fuel Company (where she worked closely with the union), also was assistant secretary of the treasury under President Franklin Delano Roosevelt. A strong New Dealer, she opposed Ed Johnson in the 1934 Democratic primary for governor but lost. *Courtesy Colorado Historical Society, Denver.*

Carrie Bella, a parachute jumper with the Rocky Mountain Flyers, at Denver Union Airport, ca. 1925. Women in the twenties found more doors opening but still had a long way to go to achieve equality. *Courtesy Colorado Historical Society, Denver.*

Early oil shale work at DeBeque. The first oil shale boom ran from 1915 to 1925. Henry Brown (right) used the oil in medicines, but there was a wide variety of marketing schemes. Oil shale has ruined many a dream in the twentieth century. *Courtesy Colorado Historical Society, Denver.*

Coal replaced gold as Colorado's most important mining product after World War I. By the late 1920s, the aggregate value of coal mined surpassed gold, and the long-ignored coal miners could point with pride to what they had accomplished. This group of miners in Ravenwood, Huerfano County, in 1935, also reflects the ethnic diversity among miners. *Courtesy Pueblo Library District.*

In 1915 miners built this swimming pool at the Oregon and Ophir mines in Garden Gulch west of Boulder. Such an amenity was extremely rare. *Courtesy Carnegie Library, Boulder.*

Colorado had been hailed as a health resort since territorial days. The "one-lunged army" (tuberculars) came to seek a cure in the high, dry air with "plenty of ozone." Sanitariums, like this one in Colorado Springs, opened in many communities along the foothills and in the mountains. *Courtesy Colorado Springs Pioneers Museum.*

Pueblo, like other Colorado towns, suffered from occasional floods, including this one on June 2, 3, and 5, 1921. On the 5th, Schaeffer Reservoir on Beaver Creek broke through the dam. The flood has been called the most important event in Pueblo history. Nature has repeatedly shown Coloradans who is in charge. *Courtesy Pueblo Library District.*

Railroading had its dangerous moments. This wreck occurred July 18, 1929, when a bridge collapsed five miles east of Vona. *Courtesy Denver Public Library/Western History Department.*

With the coming of franchise stores, such as this Safeway in Meeker, the days of the "Mom and Pop" stores were numbered. Housewives were pleased with the greater selection and lower prices. *Courtesy Rio Blanco Historical Society and White River Museum, Meeker.*

Track improvements on the Denver & Rio Grande Western near Salida, August 1927. By now regular gauge (4' 8½") was replacing the earlier, popular narrow gauge (3'). Only on a few mountain lines did the latter survive. *Courtesy Colorado Historical Society, Denver.*

Airplane crash in downtown Colorado Springs on April 28, 1926. Denver and Colorado Springs were already tied into transcontinental routes and offered airmail service. *Courtesy Colorado College/Special Collections, Colorado Springs.*

Airplanes at Rifle, July 1925. A Douglas, two DeHavilland 4s and a Curtiss JN-4 "Jenny." The airplane promised to end the isolation that had hampered much of Colorado since the Pike's Peak rush. Reality, however, fell short of expectations. *Courtesy Colorado Historical Society, Denver.*

Norwegian-born Carl Howelsen had a major impact on the development of skiing in Colorado. The ski area that he developed at Steamboat Springs still boasts Howelsen Hill, one of the major ski jumps in the United States. *Courtesy Routt County Historical Collection/Bud Werner Memorial Library, Steamboat Springs.*

Baseball has long been popular in Colorado. Las Animas's Japanese team in 1928 was one of the ethnic nines that helped immigrants enter America's mainstream. *Courtesy Pueblo Library District.*

As this 1929 photograph shows, Mesa Verde National Park was already becoming crowded with automobiles. The visitors are lined up in front of the museum awaiting the start of a ranger-conducted automobile tour. *Courtesy Mesa Verde National Park.*

The old West was alive and well in rodeos and tourist attractions. Popular motion pictures also glamorized a legendary time and place. Fort
Morgan County Fair, ca. 1915. *Courtesy Fort Morgan Museum.*

Watermelon Day in Rocky Ford. Most towns had some kind of a festival to bring the community together and lure visitors. *Photo by Harry Buckwalter. Courtesy Colorado Historical Society, Denver.*

Because of the interest in travel to the mountains, the Trinidad Chamber of Commerce operated a public park at Stonewall on land donated by the Colorado Fuel and Iron Company. By the 1920s most Colorado communities hoped to tap the tourist trade. *Courtesy Pueblo Library District.*

Family camping outfit in Genesee Park, 1919. Denver welcomed tourists from the start and emerged as the most popular destination point. Bicyclists had first called for good roads; now automobilists demanded them. *Courtesy Denver Public Library/Western History Department.*

Dedication of Rocky Mountain National Park at Horseshoe Park, September 4, 1915. Thanks to the efforts of Enos Mills and his supporters, Colorado had two national parks. The new park soon far surpassed the more isolated Mesa Verde in popularity. Mills stands second from left; next to him are Estes Park hotel owner F. O. Stanley (with flag), Representative Edward Taylor (center), and Governor George Carlson (right). *Courtesy Fort Collins Public Library.*

When grizzly bears still roamed the Colorado Rockies, these two hunters posed with their trophy in the Montrose area. In the 1990s Coloradans are debating proposals to reintroduce grizzlies. *Courtesy Montrose County Historical Society, Montrose.*

The Depression was bad enough — then the Plains states became a dust bowl. A dust storm at Holly in the early 1930s. *Courtesy Colorado Historical Society, Denver.*

The sky was dark at noon, farms were abandoned, and families relocated as the dust storms swept eastern Colorado. A farm near Pueblo is shown here. *Courtesy Pueblo Library District.*

Depression, dust, low prices — and then grasshoppers. A farmer surveys crop destruction caused by grasshoppers in Lincoln County, 1934. The 1930s would be long remembered by those who lived through them. *Photo by E. K. Edward and Son. Courtesy Colorado Historical Society, Denver.*

Using a horse to seine suckers in the Colorado River at Thompson's Ranch near Hot Sulphur Springs, ca. 1930. This method could produce great quantities of suckers, which were canned for winter use. During the Depression, Coloradans were forced into such efforts for food and work. *Courtesy Grand County Museum, Hot Sulphur Springs.*

"Hoovervilles" or "Jungle Towns," which housed the unemployed, were all too common in Colorado. This one in Pueblo during the Depression, ca. 1938, was typical. Wood, tin, cardboard, and paper shacks predominated. *Photo by Works Progress Administration. Courtesy Pueblo Library District.*

Results of a rabbit hunt in eastern Colorado during the Depression. Rabbits were hunted to save crops and rangeland, and the meat provided some needed income. *Courtesy Fort Morgan Museum.*

Works Progress Administration sewing project met in this Littleton building during the New Deal. New Deal projects employed Coloradans from all walks of life. *Photo by Gressinger. Courtesy Littleton Historical Museum.*

Governor Ed Johnson tried a controversial plan to ease the state's unemployment crisis: stop out-of-work people at the border and send them back home. Colorado National Guardsmen ordered these travelers out of their car for questioning and a search under martial law on April 21, 1936. Scores of people were stopped and many were sent back to New Mexico. *Photo by the* Denver Post. *Courtesy Colorado Historical Society, Denver.*

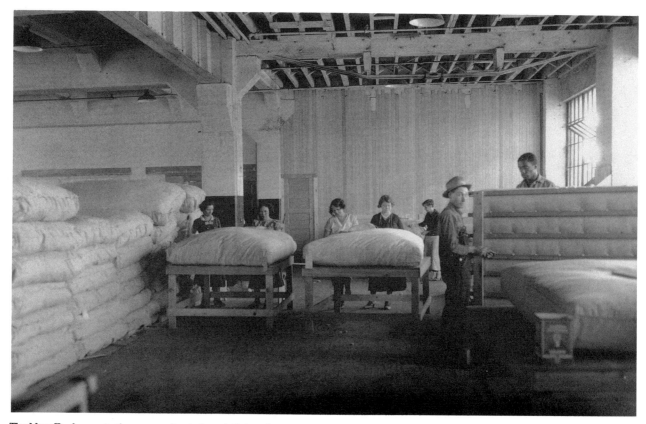

The New Deal came to the rescue of out-of-work Coloradans in a variety of ways. This Federal Emergency Relief Administration mattress factory employed many people. *Courtesy Colorado State Archives, Denver.*

When the price of gold was raised to $35 per ounce, the hills tempted a new breed of miners. Old skills, however, were gone. This Works Progress Administration project taught gold panning on the Platte River, ca. 1934. *Photo by George Perrin. Courtesy Englewood Public Library.*

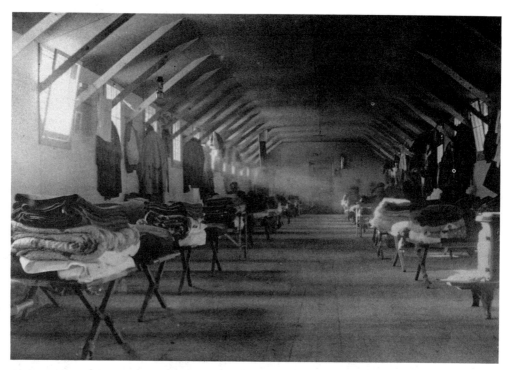

CCC barracks at Colorado National Monument. The boys signed up for six-month tours and received medical, educational, and social benefits as well as a job. *Courtesy Colorado National Monument, Grand Junction.*

Colorado National Monument CCC crew. Most camps of the New Deal Civilian Conservation Corps were segregated, but several in Colorado housed blacks, Hispanics, and Anglos. Young men were paid $30 per month, $25 of which had to be sent home. *Photo by John Schutte. Courtesy Frontier Historical Society, Glenwood Springs.*

Baseball has always been popular in Colorado, perhaps reaching its pre–World War II peak with the annual *Denver Post* tournament. Some of the country's premier black teams appeared in it; this is Denver's first black semi-pro team, the 1930 White Elephants. *Courtesy Denver Public Library/Western History Department.*

Among the players of the 1936 *Denver Post* tournament were these three all-time black stars. The Negro All-Stars won that year. *Courtesy Jay Sanford, Arvada.*

Byron "Whizzer" White of Wellingon became the University of Colorado's first All-American football player in 1937. More important, White graduated first in his class and was a Rhodes scholar. He was appointed to the U.S. Supreme Court in 1962. *Photo by Charles Snow. Courtesy University of Colorado/Western Historical Collections, Boulder.*

Colorado National Guard war games, August 1938. By the late 1930s the world was back to war talk and preparations. Europe marched to war in September 1939, and America turned its industry and agriculture to war-related needs. The Depression slipped into history. *Photo by the* Denver Post. *Courtesy Colorado Historical Society, Denver.*

IV

WELCOME TO THE NEW COLORADO
1941–1970

"JAPAN STARTED IT. The United States will finish it," headlined the *Denver Post* on December 8, 1941. An editorial in the next day's *Montrose Daily Press* was less passionate and more reasoned. Although the method of attack had stirred "the American people into a state of frenzy," the editor concluded that they "have the will to make enormous sacrifices [to protect] their own shores, [themselves], and their interests." Coloradans, in the next four years, would make those sacrifices and irrevocably alter their state and themselves. No other single event in the state's history, or any other national crisis — not the Civil War, Leadville, Cripple Creek, the silver issue, World War I, or the 1930s depression — brought so many major changes to Colorado.

One impact came from the sheer manpower needed to conduct the war — slightly over 138,800 men and women enlisted or were drafted into the armed forces. Of these, approximately 2,700 died from battle wounds and other causes. Nearly one-eighth of the state's population served in the military. Hardly any family in Colorado was unaffected by the demands of war.

Statistics are easy to enumerate. Not so easily recaptured are the heartache produced by broken homes and dire messages from the War Department; the waiting and working for the momentous events termed V-E and V-J days; the increasing anxiety over news from the various fronts as the war progressed; the ration books and limited consumer goods (such as gasoline, tires, sugar) — all the daily fears and frustrations that accompany modern warfare. Because transportation was restricted, families tended to stay at home to grow victory gardens and support local paper and scrap metal drives (the latter caused nineteenth-century mining remains to virtually disappear), Red Cross activities, and book collections for the troops.

It is hard to recapture now all the ways this war affected the lives of Coloradans. Aspen's mayor warned all citizens to be "on the lookout for acts of sabotage" (*Aspen Times*, December 18, 1941), and the newspaper advised its readers to buy defense bonds and stamps. The *Pagosa Springs Sun* recommended severe penalties for violators of the wartime thirty-five-miles-per-hour speed limit (June 25, 1943). According to the *Meeker Herald*, the watchword was "Save"; the February 3, 1944, issue featured an article on waste paper, which ranked with iron, aluminum, steel, and rubber as one of the essentials for winning the war. Then came the news that everyone had been waiting for: the May 8, 1945, *Denver Post* announced, "ALLIED VICTORY PROCLAIMED; Denver greets victory with thankfulness." Coloradans were even more thankful when the Japanese surrendered that September.

The state's economy expanded in response to wartime demands. Mining went to war and came back changed; it also acquired a new partner in Uncle Sam. Since the early days of the New Deal, government regulation had been a fact of life. It was nothing, however, compared to what went on from 1942 to 1945. In the opinion of many miners, the most infamous act came with the Gold Limitation Order, L-280, in October 1942. This closed nonessential mineral mines by denying mine operators access to replacement materials and forbidding work other than maintenance. Its purpose was to free miners and equipment for mines that produced war-critical metals and fuels. Gold and silver mines closed; for the first time since the 1890s, Cripple Creek fell nearly silent.

In order to focus the war effort, the government involved itself in all phases of mining. From conducting research (oil shale, uranium, and war-related minerals) to building roads, from deferring and relocating miners to establishing prices, Washington invaded what had been the sacred domain of the industry. The old-time prospectors would have been aghast at Uncle Sam's audacious new role in mining. But many contemporary miners didn't mind. Across the state, mining necessary for the war prospered. Moffat, La Plata, Weld, and Las Animas counties, for example, increased coal production to record tonnages in some cases. Above Leadville, Climax Molybdenum had been gradually expanding operations since the 1920s. During the war, Colorado produced nearly all the world's supply of molybdenum, $29 million worth in 1942. Wartime needs energized the production of vanadium and oil, and in 1943–44 Colorado's greatest oil field was opened at Rangely. Northwestern Colorado had finally come into its own.

The farmer also prospered, as agriculture responded to war demands with the largest yields in the state's history. Montrose was confident that the isolated Uncompahgre Valley's agriculture and livestock production could be just as important to defense as the manufacture of war goods. The neighboring Gunnison Valley cultivated every available acre of cropland in order to meet the Food for Freedom campaign's annual quota. Labor shortages sent schoolboys and girls into the sugar beet fields near Fort Morgan to harvest the 1942 crop; teachers and students at Fort Lewis Junior College also helped reap the harvest. And similar circumstances abounded across Colorado.

The agricultural boom continued for several years after the war; it had been decades since the farmer and rancher had fared so well. Yet their numbers continued to dwindle as they had throughout the century. Increased mechanization accounted for part of this attrition, certainly, but so did the age-old attraction of the cities and their better-paying jobs.

Colorado industry was also converted to supply wartime necessities. Hardly an industrial plant in the state, from the large Colorado Fuel and Iron to the small family-run factories, remained untouched. The variety of war goods they produced was impressive — barges, knives, aircraft parts, ammunition, bombs, tires, boilers, medicines, chemicals, and even ships were built in land-locked Denver. The Denver Ordnance Plant, begun in 1941, was perhaps Colorado's most important industrial producer. At its peak it employed almost 20,000 and emerged as one of the largest establishments of its kind in the nation.

Federal money also flowed to construct a Japanese relocation center near Granada in the southeastern part of the state. In the immediate post–Pearl Harbor hysteria, Japanese on the West Coast had been rounded up and placed in camps; then the government decided to move them to more isolated sites. Many of the political leaders in the Rocky Mountain states, including Senator Ed Johnson, opposed a move to this area (Greeley's city council voted unanimously to oppose any resettlement in its vicinity), but Governor Ralph Carr came to the aid of the internees and took a stand against fear and racist thinking: "No governor has the right to deny to any American citizen, or any person living within the country legally, the right to enter or to reside in or cross his state." The result was the Granada Relocation Center at Amache; at least two-thirds of its residents were American citizens. Said to be the tenth-largest city in Colorado when it reached its full population in 1942 (7,500), Amache was surrounded by over 10,000 acres of desolate prairie, which its residents converted into profitable farmland. Though it started from scratch, the community proved highly successful in farming and business. However, animosity toward the Japanese did not die, despite the success of Amache. In some ways it raged more hotly because of it. This episode revealed one of the more contemptible sides of

Coloradans, and of Americans in general, as they reacted to World War II. Amache was closed in 1945 and eventually overtaken by the prairie from which it had arisen.

Colorado's future was changed by a host of other developments that came to pass during 1941–45. Military installations brought hundreds of thousands of young men and women into the state, many of whom wished to return when the war was over. And many did. They were stationed at Lowry Air Field, Buckley Field, Peterson Air Field, Pueblo Army Air Base, and two posts that had particularly important impacts, Camp Hale and Camp Carson, soon to be Fort Carson.

The largest of these, Fort Carson near Colorado Springs, trained more than 150,000 men. Flush times and a military flavor came to Colorado Springs with the infusion of federal money and military installations. Most of the influx came during the war, but some facilities were brought in afterward, including the North American Air Defense Command. Camp Hale, northwest of Leadville, became the practice site for ski troops to learn specialized combat techniques; these units evolved into the famous Tenth Mountain Division. They trained for two years (in one war game they surrendered their camp and much of central Colorado!) before being sent to a bloody campaign in Italy. Members of the Tenth would remember their training location as some of Colorado's greatest skiing territory and would return after the war to help build up the ski industry at Aspen and Vail.

The state's colleges and universities also implemented wartime training programs. The University of Colorado housed a language school for the Navy, and Colorado A&M a quartermaster unit, for instance. At the end of the war, thanks to the GI Bill and renewed interest in higher education, the opportunities for schooling expanded and transformed Colorado. They would also present the legislature with an ongoing money crisis.

Perhaps no other place was more affected by World War II than Denver. Like most American cities, Denver became familiar with air raid rules, rationing, price controls, conservation of gasoline, and scrap drives, but it also harbored more government agencies (moved inland to keep them away from possible enemy attack) and received more defense dollars than any other community in the state. Residents had to get used to low-altitude practice flights over the city by Lowry pilots and a downtown crowded by some four million servicewomen and men passing through. All the disruptions had their compensations, though. Growth and prosperity returned and revitalized Denver. The city that now sprawls along the foothills is largely the product of this war and the two decades that followed it.

The economic spurt created by the war years was clearly evident in Colorado's population, which jumped 200,000 to 1.3 million–plus during the 1940s, a greater increase than any other Rocky Mountain state except Arizona. Service personnel had indeed fallen in love with Colorado, and the economic revival created the jobs for them and others to fill. The growth, mainly urban, spread out along the Eastern Slope. Denver and the three adjacent counties — Adams, Arapahoe, and Jefferson — accounted for 78 percent of that growth. People migrated in huge numbers to the strip between Fort Collins and Colorado Springs and revolutionized Colorado's future. The census of 1950 revealed that thirty-five out of the sixty-three counties had actually lost population, most of it to the Eastern Slope foothills area. The mountain and eastern plains counties experienced especially heavy losses, a disturbing trend. For the moment, at least, the rural areas still controlled the legislature, but rural Colorado was definitely going on the defensive as the 1950s opened.

Politically, economically, and commercially, Denver dominated the rest of the state more than it had since the nineteenth century. The federal infusion of jobs, agencies, and money, and the Front Range urbanization, brought a higher standard of living, an incursion of highly skilled workers, and altered political, social, and cultural attitudes. By 1960 Denver had 493,000 residents and was surrounded by fast-growing suburbs. It was also facing the same problems as any other twentieth-century American big city — traffic congestion, crime, smog, a limited tax base, growing racial tensions, and a decline of downtown business.

Newspaperman, writer, and poet Thomas Hornsby Ferril spoke for many of his fellow Denverites when he deplored the city's growing crime problem. After he and his wife were threatened by "two young hoodlums," he exploded in *The Rocky Mountain Herald*, "But whatever long-range ideas we have toward trying to solve these insoluble problems, there's the immediate problem of preserving law and order and isolating dangerous people right now" (August 1, 1964). Denver had become a part of twentieth-century urban America.

Postwar Colorado was an exciting place to be. For the next two decades, the "sell Colorado" theme, resurrected from earlier days, played a prominent role among the state's movers and shakers. Businesses swarmed to Denver and the suburbs, as well as to outlying towns along the Front Range urban strip. The climate, scenery, and less-crowded conditions appealed to a variety of corporations, from the Hilton Hotel chain to Martin Marietta and IBM. Another factor that lured big business to the state was the relative weakness of organized labor, which had never recovered from the violent clashes at the turn of the century; most of the work force was non-unionized. Around the workers and their jobs sprang up housing projects, described by one historian as an "architectural fungus" that produced visual monotony. The suburbs grew faster than Denver, jeopardizing the city's future; its affluent citizens followed the high-paying jobs. One city's gain was another's loss.

The state also found itself a vital player in the cold war between communist and free world nations. No more would the Rocky Mountain region be isolated from the developments occurring around it; the world was shrinking. The Atomic Energy Commission's Rocky Flats plant, which manufactured components for nuclear weapons, went into operation near Denver. More significantly, Colorado produced uranium, a product needed by both sides as they armed themselves with the latest warheads. The world had attained the atomic era.

Uranium kicked off Colorado's last great mining rush. Though hauntingly familiar, it was yet strikingly different from the ones that had come before. The late 1940s and 1950s brought some exciting times to the vast, rugged, dry land of plateaus and canyons in western Colorado. Activity revolved around Grand Junction, but Rifle, Uravan, Rico, Slick Rock, Maybell, Durango, Naturita, and other communities also prospered. Replacing the burro and mining pan in this rush to riches were jeeps, Geiger counters, and low-flying airplanes. "Uranium has become a magic word for many Americans in the past few years," claimed the guidebook *Uranium: Where It Is and How to Find It*, which emphasized how anybody could become rich with a uranium claim or two.

The rush received national attention. Over 100 uranium companies in Grand Junction alone, and a higher number of promoters, enticed American investors to catch the fever. Penny stocks allowed everyone to speculate. Those who wanted to delve into serious mining sought out the nearest dry goods store that had a "Prospectors' Corner," where books, supplies (relatively heavy clothes and an air mattress were recommended items), and other paraphernalia tempted them.

For all the likenesses of this rush to its predecessors, there was one major difference: the Atomic Energy Commission was superintending it all. It sponsored road-building programs, paid bonuses for production, purchased ore, and imposed a variety of regulations to control this mining so vital to America's and the Western world's defense. From 1948 through 1960 Colorado produced $133 million worth of uranium ore before production slowed down. In the sixties the AEC began to curtail its support and limit its purchases when it had stockpiled enough for immediate needs. By 1969 uranium production had fallen to barely a third of what it had been ten years before. The uranium boom was over. A degree of quiet returned to the plateau country, scarred now by the dumps, roads going nowhere, and relics left by the prospectors and miners who had passed that way. The uranium rush also left behind another legacy: the strange properties of the ore itself. The threat posed by radioactive wastes — tailings piled at mill sites or used as fill in construction projects at Grand Junction — would eventually be understood. The miners who had worked in the mines, breathing radon gas and coming into repeated contact with the "hot" ores, would experience serious health problems down the line.

The postwar Colorado oil boom, which paralleled the uranium activity, received less publicity but produced more wealth. The Rangely Field developed into one of the world's major oil regions. It was followed in the early fifties by the opening of the Denver-Julesburg basin, which overlapped the earlier Boulder–Fort Collins discoveries. At the same time, La Plata County came into prominence with both oil and natural gas. The state's crude oil production rose steadily until it reached a peak of 58 million barrels in 1956. Though it seemed like the royal road to wealth, the oil business proved fickle and the driller faced high odds. For example, of the 1,539 oil and gas wells drilled in 1955, 1,043 were dry.

Counties that had known little or no previous mineral activity were suddenly swept into the middle of the boom. Farmers and ranchers in Logan and Morgan counties watched the oil men elbow their way onto the scene. Wide, unbroken, high-plains vistas were now framed by derricks and storage tanks. In Morgan County the population rose 22 percent in seven years. La Plata County followed a similar path, and Durango prospered when it became the oil companies' headquarters. Mining entered a new era, founded on the old standby of molybdenum, along with oil and uranium, which replaced the gold, silver, and coal of earlier generations. The industry's impact on the environment was beginning to stir people's consciences. A generation hence that issue would have a great impact on mining activities.

In the high mountain valleys where hard-rock mining once prospered, a new kind of boom was touched off by skiing. Colorado, which would later hail itself as "Ski Country, U.S.A.," had finally found the perfect complement to its summer tourism attractions — a popular winter recreation. From southwestern Colorado through the central Rockies to Vail and Steamboat Springs, ski areas were opened or revitalized, attracting locals and spreading the word of

Colorado's dry, powdery snow and widely acclaimed runs. Skiers came in droves, until the popular slopes experienced overcrowding. One reporter noted in 1969, "Thousands of people were in Vail . . . they were tumbling down the mountains themselves as if the whole of Chicago and Minneapolis had been parachuted into the Rockies."

New ski resorts, such as Vail and Purgatory, opened for business in the 1960s as more investors rushed to cash in on the popularity of the sport. The old silver town of Aspen witnessed one of the most interesting developments. Here skiing was combined with culture to revive a community left over from another era. Some of the Tenth Mountain boys played a major role in this innovation, but the real mover and shaker was Chicago manufacturer Walter Paepcke. As he explained, "When I saw Aspen, I wasn't just thinking of starting a place that would attract tourists. Here was a town . . . [that] possessed all the attributes of a wonderful place to live." He helped turn Aspen into a health, sports, and cultural center that featured, among other things, a summer music festival.

All this development was not done without some complaints and disruption. Old-timers groused about the inevitable changes. One complained to a writer for the *Reporter*, "I'm for all Walter has done for this town. But we're still hoping to bring in something more substantial" (August 8, 1957). Uranium was what he had in mind. He and his friends were doomed, because Aspen was on the road to fame and celebrity; many visitors who saw it and Denver in the sixties believed they had seen all of Colorado.

Telluride went through similar changes, but later. Mining did not give way graciously to skiing and tourism. Old-timers there were antagonized by the influx of the long-haired-hippy element. The newcomers became so bold as to attack mining as a polluter and a destroyer of the environment. Times were not happy at Telluride. The old guard fought a losing rear guard action to preserve its way of life; the once-forgotten mining community became an all-season resort catering to vacationers. Central City knew all about this kind of thing — it had already sold out its heritage. As the mayor said to a *Newsweek* reporter, "We still get the gold. We get it from some 450,000 tourists a year" (July 26, 1954).

Colorado tourism got a tremendous boost when popular President Dwight Eisenhower chose to vacation in the state and fish for the "wily trout." Ike, whose wife Mamie was a Denver native, had enjoyed Colorado over the years, and the picture of the beaming president holding a string of fresh-caught trout did wonders for promotion. When he suffered a heart attack while in the state in 1955, Colorado tourism endured a temporary setback.

Although not intended as such, another major tourist attraction came to

Colorado in the 1950s. The June 24, 1954, Colorado Springs *Gazette Telegraph* headlined the achievement: "SPRINGS GETS ACADEMY." The article went on to say, "One of the biggest gambles ever undertaken by the Colorado Springs Chamber of Commerce paid off with stupendous odds today." More than a gamble, it had been a concerted effort by the whole state, and it reaped a handsome reward. Colorado had been in competition for several years with other states and sites to win this prize. By 1954 the contest was limited to three finalists. Colorado offered a million dollars toward the purchase of the land, along with roads; Colorado Springs would supply water, and the private sector held out other inducements. It was an example of statewide cooperation at its best. The offer was accepted, and bulldozers and earth movers were soon at work. Lowry served as the temporary campus until August 1958, when the Cadet Wing moved into the new academy buildings. The facility very quickly brought national attention to the state and became a favorite stopping place for tourists. Colorado could not have made a better investment.

In these postwar decades the tourist industry became important to almost all Colorado communities, emerging as one of the state's major economic foundations. The construction of the interstate highway system proved vital to tourism but deadly to those small towns, especially the ones on the eastern plains, that found themselves bypassed. Longtime favorite destinations, such as Rocky Mountain and Mesa Verde national parks, grew steadily in popularity, until by the 1960s fear was expressed that they could be "loved to death." On summer days tourists crowded in and hurried to visit all the attractions in an environment that was not ideally suited to that kind of pressure. Debates and studies ensued to determine just what the government's policy should be. The national forests also came under scrutiny, particularly as the concept of multiple use was developed and various interests clashed over who should have priority.

Towns close to these and other scenic areas prospered by their proximity. Old mining towns jump-started their sputtering economies when many Americans came to enjoy four-wheel drives in the mountains and visits to old mine sites. Hinsdale County, for one, depended on tourists for its very existence. Central City's opera season enhanced that community immensely, as did its nearness to Denver, still one of the major destination points for tourists. Coloradans could even point with pride to their own opera, "The Ballad of Baby Doe," which premiered at Central City in 1956; once more the Tabors came to center stage. Other old mining towns, such as Cripple Creek with its melodrama, lured a share of the tourist trade. Tourist blessings were showered on Durango and Silverton, which capitalized on Americans' love affair with steam trains.

The narrow-gauge trip between the two towns, following the Animas Canyon in the heart of the San Juans, became a must for many visitors.

While travelers relaxed and enjoyed the sights, the people who lived in Colorado year-round struggled to resolve a variety of issues. The state's educational system, from elementary through college, was expanding steadily, putting great pressure on the state's finances. Education became the major item in the budget; money could not be found for all the programs and groups that wanted it. Each had its own agenda, and the hard-pressed legislators had fewer and fewer options.

If growth and development were what Coloradans wanted during these decades — and all evidence pointed to the fact that the majority did — then water held the key to achieving them. But water was becoming a complicated and emotional issue, as neighboring states proposed their own plans. The upper and lower basins were still arguing over the Colorado River; finally, in 1956, Congress authorized the Upper Colorado River projects. They included plans for more dams, reservoirs, and power plants, but the main purpose was to achieve equitable division and apportionment of water. Some projects were completed; others still languish on the drawing boards nearly forty years later. State jealousies and sectional interests heightened as each state sought to protect its own future. At the end of the 1960s, the amazing growth of southern California and the Phoenix area placed new demands on old compacts and gave the lower basin states enough power to outgun the upper basin states in politics and in Congress.

Another intrastate water project, the Frying Pan–Arkansas, was approved in 1962. It collected and transported water across the Continental Divide to partly satisfy the growing thirst of the Eastern Slope. Once again Western Slopers protested the diversion; nevertheless, the project was completed. Water flows toward money, as Coloradans and others were discovering in no uncertain terms. Politically and financially, the urban corridor had the clout to bring about the metamorphosis it desired.

The 1960s started peacefully enough, but by the end of the decade Coloradans, like other Americans, had seen their communities and their state torn apart over civil rights and the war in Vietnam. The former generally involved Hispanics; from Denver to Center in the San Luis Valley, they pushed for the acceptance and recognition that so often had been denied them in a world where they were described as "with us, but not of us." In Denver Rodolfo "Corky" Gonzales organized the Crusade for Justice, which tackled a broad spectrum of Latin- and Mexican-American problems. The group held meetings, sponsored a Poor People's March to demand that neighborhood school boards control local schools and public housing, and even organized a political party.

In Center the first priority was education as Hispanic parents for the first time involved themselves on a large scale, advocating better treatment for their children and celebration of Mexican Independence Day, among other things. Cries of "Chicano power!" were heard in a community that was 60 percent Hispanic but completely controlled by Anglos. Center provided a clear example of the problems Hispanics confronted — and it was not an isolated one. All across Colorado, communities were dealing with the same issues. The Hispanic population was growing during the 1960s (it more than doubled in Denver, to 17 percent of the city's total), and its advocates were becoming more vocal. Although they did not immediately achieve all they were striving for, they forced the Anglo majority to listen and become more sensitive to cultural and ethnic differences.

Blacks, too, made strides. Colorado's black population was concentrated largely in Denver — the census of 1970 found more than two-thirds of the state's 66,411 black residents living there. Since World War II they had made steady economic and educational gains, but integration into traditionally white neighborhoods was not one of them. Denver had been transformed into an island of ethnic minorities and poor people and old people, surrounded by a sea of middle-class white families. The white exodus to the suburbs had been noticeable for years. Blacks would begin fighting for integration with school busing in the next decade, although Denver voters turned their backs on school candidates who supported busing in a 1969 election. Even so, Denver came to grips with racial issues much better than many other large cities at that time.

Colorado's Indians, unlike the blacks and Hispanics, were concentrated in three areas: the Ute Mountain Ute and Southern Ute reservations in the southwestern corner of the state, and in the capital city. Denver's 4,000-plus Indians migrated into the city mostly from the northern Plains reservations. They found the life difficult to adjust to and their incomes generally much lower than other ethnic groups. The Southern Utes, on the other hand, bridged the gap between the cultures (Ignacio, their center, was tri-ethnic) and adapted economically and socially to the world around them. They became aware, nonetheless, that they were losing their own culture, and by the end of the sixties they were making a concerted effort to preserve it. Life for the more conservative Ute Mountain Utes was much more difficult on their isolated and poverty-ridden reservation at Towaoc, south of Cortez; for them the road was much harder.

Minorities constituted one explosive issue, the Vietnam War another. The opposition to it began on college campuses and in the homes of war opponents, then spread to the streets and onto the nation's nightly news programs. Young Colorado men sought ways to avoid the draft, students protested, demonstrators marched. The debate split Coloradans, creating anger and dissension that raised questions about democracy, education, government, and the American character. In this respect, Colorado and the Rocky Mountain states were no different from other regions. Vietnam created mistrust and hatred, both of which carried over into the next decade.

Politically, the state remained primarily conservative during the quarter of a century after World War II. The Republican party held the reins of power most of that time, particularly in the state legislature, although the Democrats won the governor's chair more times than not in the 1950s. John Love, a Colorado clone of the popular Eisenhower, led a Republican resurgence, winning the governorship in 1962 and in the next two elections. Starting with the 1958 election, terms were four years. Colorado was growing, and that was important to Love and his supporters, who believed it was vital to the state's future. But with that growth came more demands on the Colorado budget, from prisons to education. The governor and the legislature squared off over who held the purse strings, the latter gradually gaining ascendancy.

One of the most critical political problems lay in the fact that growth and prosperity were concentrated primarily in the urban areas, but the heritage from the nineteenth century put control of the legislature in rural hands. Misunderstanding and lack of communication too often fouled debate and thwarted legislative action. The rural areas feared that if they ever let go of their power, their doom was sealed, because city legislators could be just as indifferent and unsympathetic to rural issues as rural legislators had sometimes been to urban issues. The struggle became one between past and future. When the U.S. Supreme Court finally ruled "one man, one vote," the issue was decided. It would take years, however, before the 100-seat Colorado House and Senate truly reflected the demographic patterns. The future would be in the hands of the elected delegates from the densely populated area that stretched from Fort Collins to Pueblo.

Those Coloradans weary of pondering weighty public problems could divert their attention to a favorite sports team. College football and basketball had their fans; the University of Colorado, Colorado State University, and the Air Force Academy all underwrote big-time athletics. Even more exciting was the fact that Colorado was entering the age of professional sports. Denver had had minor league baseball for some time. In 1960 major league football made its debut with the Denver Broncos. The hope was that the Broncos would serve to advertise the city and the state, thus attracting industry, investment, and people. Some may have questioned the logic of all these expectations as the Broncos endured one losing season after another. Coaches and players came and went, but nothing seemed to work. Nevertheless, the fans remained loyal, crowding Mile High Stadium on Sunday afternoons. The Denver Rockets came on the scene later in the decade to give the city another franchise, this one in the American Basketball Association.

Professional sports displayed the positive side of the growth equation. Ever since 1858 Coloradans had been caught up in the "grow or die" syndrome. Now, however, a growing minority was questioning the wisdom of the idea, generally focusing on the impact of growth on the state's environment. That environment in and of itself bestowed an economic advantage. Boulder emerged as one of the leaders in the fight to preserve it, as the town with the picturesque and distinguished university and the foothills setting became a mecca for new residents. Citizens there organized and protested until, at the end of the 1960s, the city had in place a "greenbelt" plan to buy land to maintain open space. Other activists favored limited development and a cap on the population size. These policies, heresies in an earlier generation, now seemed rational to a growing number of people.

Boulder was not the only community that evidenced active environmental concern. Residents along Clear Creek vehemently attacked the dumping of untreated sewage into the stream by Black Hawk and Central City; towns in other areas of the state, such as Silverton, Minturn, and Redcliff, were criticized for the same offense. Polluters used a plea of poverty to delay action. Various kinds of environmental pollution also came from active and inactive mines and from summer residents, tourists, Denver, and just about everywhere and everybody else. The *Denver Post, Rocky Mountain News*, and other papers sought to raise Coloradans' awareness. They editorialized about water pollution, air pollution, the destruction of the South Platte River (which had become a "moving cesspool"), and trash — "Will it bury us?" the *Post* wondered in a December 9, 1969, article. The writer pointed out that Coloradans created four tons of trash per minute, 240 tons per hour, and that it would cost nearly $30 million per year to handle it properly, an amount that obviously was not being spent. Within a year the same paper suggested that the three traditional concepts — population growth, economic growth, and dependence on the automobile — would have to be changed if Coloradans were to preserve their "quality of life."

Thomas Hornsby Ferril had questioned the idea of growth a decade before in the February 21, 1959, issue of *The Rocky Mountain Herald:* "As an elder sentimentalist, I keep telling myself how much more I enjoyed Denver when it was smaller." With life becoming "more uncomfortable and inconvenient," he posed the question that more of his contemporaries would soon ask: "Why has expansion alone come to be synonymous with the good life?"

Maintaining the quality of life was not a new idea — it had been around since the first miners, farmers, and camp denizens had settled along the streams. As the years went by, that quality deteriorated, with the automobile receiving most of the attention as a major villain by the 1960s. Coloradans had become enamored of the gasoline-powered vehicle — they owned an average of nearly two per family, turning the skies brown with car exhaust along the Front Range. Coloradans had also been prone to littering since the beginning of the territory's existence. The difference between then and now could be explained by the fact that the nineteenth century's junk was the twentieth century's valued antique, which was carried pridefully home by treasure-seekers who left behind their own junk — pop cans and paper sacks — to mark their trail.

Much of the charm of the state was being threatened, along with the tourist business. Aspen, Grand Lake, Manitou Springs, and other popular tourist spots were already facing crises brought on by too much popularity. Solutions to these questions of environment and pollution were not easy to come by. Auguring well for the future was the rising awareness, interest, and activity being directed toward the problem. Under reevaluation was the maxim that growth should serve as the yardstick against which to measure community and state progress. It was obvious that some compromises would have to be made if the exciting prospects of the 1970s were to be realized. Colorado now mirrored the rest of the country more than it ever had before, but it was also taking steps in new directions.

Governor Ralph Carr of Antonito registers for the draft with Ruth Kennedy of the draft board, April 27, 1942. Carr would soon become famous for his support of the Japanese-Americans. *Photo by the* Denver Post. *Courtesy Colorado Historical Society, Denver.*

War bonds, gas rationing, scrap drives, victory gardens — they were all part of Coloradans' lives during World War II. On war footing by 1940, America went to war on December 8, 1941, after the attack on Pearl Harbor. *Courtesy Tom Noel, Denver.*

Working on ship parts at the Thompson Pipe and Steel Company in Denver during World War II. The plant prefabricated amphibious landing craft for the military. *Courtesy Colorado Historical Society, Denver.*

The shift ends at the Denver Ordnance Plant in 1941. This Remington plant made ammunition, while the Rocky Mountain Arsenal produced bombs. Lowry Air Field, Buckley Field, and other Colorado military installations were established during the war. *Courtesy Denver Public Library/Western History Department.*

Japanese-Americans leave the train for transport to the Granada Relocation Center at Amache, August 28, 1942. The imprisonment of American citizens without due process troubled the conscience of the nation for decades, finally leading to the acknowledgment of wrongdoing and payment of reparations. Some 7,500 were interned here at one point. *Photo by Tom Parker, War Relocation Authority. Courtesy Colorado Historical Society, Denver.*

Dairy farm foreman J. Abe at the Granada Relocation Center at Amache. While many Japanese-American men, women, and children were placed in such camps, others served with distinction in the military. *Photo by Tom Parker, War Relocation Authority. Courtesy Colorado Historical Society, Denver.*

Camp Hale, September 1943. Mountain troops learned survival skills from arctic explorer Dr. Vilhjalmur Stefansson and lived in the snowfields at elevations of up to 13,000 feet. Other important military facilities were Camp Carson (later Fort Carson) and Peterson Air Field near Colorado Springs; military bases also were located at Pueblo, La Junta, and Denver. Many of the men and women who served at these posts returned to Colorado to live after the war. *Photo by United States Signal Corps. Courtesy Colorado Historical Society, Denver.*

Conquering the obstacle course at Camp Hale, 1943. In 1944 the Tenth Mountain Division fought bravely in the Italian campaign, losing 992 men. *Courtesy U.S. Army Military History Research Collection, Carlisle Barracks, Pennsylvania.*

The all-girl marching band at the University of Colorado, 1942. During the war, female college students in the state managed victory gardens, sold war bonds, and kept the marching band in business. *Photo by Floyd Walters. University of Colorado/Western Historical Collections, Boulder.*

Women in war work in Fort Collins area, April 1944. Having proven, once again, that they could handle "men's work," women were not going to return to the "good old days." *Courtesy Colorado State University/Photographic Archives, Fort Collins.*

World War II scrap drive in Craig. Even two cannons from the courthouse grounds were donated to the war effort. *Photo by George Welch.*
Courtesy Museum of Northwest Colorado, Craig.

World War II victory garden at Colorado College, 1944. Coloradans from all walks of life pitched in to win the war. *Courtesy Colorado College Special Collections, Colorado Springs.*

Colorado College women selling war-bond stamps during World War II. Known as "Minute Maids," they did such related work as donating blood, working in victory gardens and hospitals, and selling war bonds. *Courtesy Colorado College Special Collections, Colorado Springs.*

World War II Navy V-12 training on the Colorado College campus. Most campuses housed such training programs. *Courtesy Colorado College Special Collections, Colorado Springs.*

In November 1944, heavy snows forced these Littleton voters to take the tractor to the polls. *Courtesy Littleton Historical Museum.*

Labor camp built by the U.S. Department of Agriculture on the north side of Fort Lupton, 1942. With the "boys" off to war, many employers faced labor shortages. *Photo by* Greeley Tribune. *Courtesy City of Greeley Museums.*

German prisoners of war from the Fraser camp during World War II. The man at far right was the camp blacksmith and farrier. He and one other POW lived in the woods and took care of the horses and equipment for the timber crew. He had everything ready at Crystal Creek when the teamsters arrived and then went fishing until the crew returned. *Courtesy Grand County Museum, Hot Sulphur Springs.*

Camp for German prisoners of war west of Greeley, 1944–45. The camp was in existence from 1942 to 1945 and was one of several such camps in Colorado. *Courtesy City of Greeley Museums.*

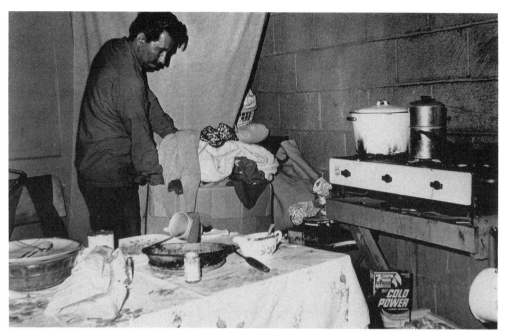

Migrant labor camp, Fort Lupton. The Colorado Department of Health forced its closing in 1969. The treatment of migratory farm workers has been a concern through much of this century. *Courtesy City of Greeley Museums.*

Telephone switchboard operators in Granby, 1949: Eleanor Bryant, Betty West, Jean Lewis, Maxine West, Shirley Hardenbrook, Marguerite Birdsell, June "Peg" Pharo, and Opal Chambers. The days of "central" were numbered even as these "girls" smiled for the camera. *Courtesy Grand County Museum, Hot Sulphur Springs.*

Police chief Jerry Boyer and Arapahoe County Sheriff E. E. Monzingo raid a bootlegger, ca. 1940s. The making of home brew has long been a Colorado pastime. *Photo by George Perrin. Courtesy Englewood Public Library.*

Fire destroyed the historic Graden building in Durango, February 17, 1948. *Photo by the* Denver Post. *Courtesy Colorado Historical Society, Denver.*

Uranium mining on the Colorado Plateau at the Woody Powell and Walt Moore mine in San Miguel County, 1950. Most such mines were small operations. The men risked dangers from radon gas and exposure to the ore. *Courtesy Museum of Western Colorado, Grand Junction.*

The Woody Powell and Walt Moore uranium mine, 1950. Typical mines were adits and stopes driven on rims of canyons or near the top of sandstone mesas. In the 1950s Colorado experienced a uranium boom, the last of its kind. *Courtesy Museum of Western Colorado, Grand Junction.*

Filming *Ticket to Tomahawk*, a 1950 film, between Durango and Silverton. Hollywood contributed to the Colorado economy during this period and attracted more tourists to see the "old West." *Photo by John L. Hake. Courtesy Adams State College, Alamosa.*

Plowing snow in the 1950s. Heavy mountain snows required major efforts to keep the rail lines open; trucks, planes, and buses severely cut into railroad traffic and profits. *Photo by John L. Hake. Courtesy Adams State College, Alamosa.*

President Dwight Eisenhower relaxing at the ranch of Aksel Nielson after fishing in the Fraser area, July 1952. Ike, an avid fly fisherman, frequently escaped to Colorado. *Courtesy Colorado Historical Society, Denver.*

Anvil Points — Bureau of Mines Oil Shale Demonstration Plant, ca. 1950s. This experimental project located just west of Rifle was dedicated in 1947. The great oil shale boom and bust came in the 1980s. *Photo by U.S. Bureau of Mines. Courtesy Colorado School of Mines, Golden, and Rifle Creek Museum, Rifle.*

Colorado Fuel, Iron and Steel helped make Pueblo the "Little Pittsburgh" of the West. It held its own for a while in the postwar years, but outside and foreign competition would take its toll. *Courtesy Pueblo Library District.*

Secretary of Agriculture Ezra Benson visits Wild Horse, Colorado. Eastern plains farmers and their towns did not enjoy the postwar growth and prosperity that brightened the lives of Front Range residents. The big new industry was skiing, which bypassed the eastern plains. *Courtesy Pueblo Library District.*

University of Colorado football arrived in the "big time" in 1957 when the team was invited to the Orange Bowl and defeated Clemson 27–21. On a fall afternoon John Wooten (69) and Bill Mondt (66) helped open a hole for Bob Stransky (20). *Courtesy University of Colorado/Athletic Department, Boulder.*

The Cotton Club on Colorado Avenue in Colorado Springs was popular with blacks and servicemen. *Courtesy Pikes Peak Library District, Colorado Springs.*

Coors — "brewed with pure Rocky Mountain spring water" — quenched the thirst of many Coloradans, then became popular across the country. By the 1980s it had expanded into a national company with plants outside of the state. Photo ca. 1960. *Courtesy Coors Brewing Company, Golden.*

Louis, Bobby, and Al Unser at the Pike's Peak Hill Climb. The Unser family is said to "own" the mountain because several generations of Unsers have dominated the event. *Courtesy Pikes Peak Library District, Colorado Springs.*

Alva Adams Paddock, better known as "Gov," was editor of Boulder's *Daily Camera*. He was one of the last of his breed, a homegrown editor and owner of the local newspaper. History and a variety of other topics absorbed Gov. *Courtesy Laurence Paddock, Boulder.*

Frank Kemp of the Great Western Sugar Company with braceros, July 8, 1960. Corporate agriculture in Colorado and elsewhere in the West sought cheap Mexican labor through the bracero program. Meanwhile, the small farmer continued to decrease in numbers and significance. *Courtesy Colorado State University, Colorado Agricultural Archives, Fort Collins.*

Lettuce harvest in the San Luis Valley, ca. 1960. Low-paid migrant workers and local residents did the physically difficult work of harvesting this crop. *Photo by Denver & Rio Grande Western. Courtesy Colorado Historical Society, Denver.*

Great Western Sugar Company employees near Fort Morgan demonstrate two different labor techniques — standing up and duck waddling. Joe Jiminez, a twenty-year employee, on the ground; Federico Juarez, ten-year employee, standing. Such farm work was very demanding physically. *Courtesy Colorado State University/Colorado Agricultural Archives, Fort Collins.*

Senator Peter Dominick and Arapahoe County Civil Defense director John Powell after a flood in Englewood in 1965, another reminder for Coloradans that they had not mastered their environment. *Courtesy Englewood Public Library.*

Paul Newman blows up the express safe in the movie *Butch Cassidy and the Sundance Kid*, filmed in the Durango area. Much to the surprise of everyone, the explosives proved too powerful and demolished the car. *Courtesy Walter Conrad, Bayfield.*

Pike's Peak Park, a Colorado Springs suburb in the 1960s. Urban sprawl had arrived! Ticky-tacky buildings, auto congestion, and the brown cloud soon touched the lives of those crowded onto the urban Front Range. *Courtesy Colorado College Special Collections, Colorado Springs.*

Modified Boeing 377 used to transport Titan missiles made by Martin Company, Stapleton Airport, October 1962. Airplanes eased the isolation from which many communities suffered, while defense contracts brightened the Colorado economy. *Photo by Gene Elliot. Courtesy Colorado Historical Society, Denver.*

Hiawatha Davis, chairman of Denver Afro-American Unity, addressing blacks at a Speak Out in Fuller Park, August 27, 1967. The 1960s and 1970s were decades of social unrest as minority groups sought better treatment. *Photo by Dennis Weiser. Courtesy Denver Public Library/Western History Department.*

Astronaut M. Scott Carpenter, a Boulder-born University of Colorado graduate, is recognized by his alma mater in 1962. Coloradans were conquering the last frontier, space. *Courtesy University of Colorado/Western Historical Collections, Boulder.*

The Boulder/Denver Turnpike changed the history and growth patterns of all the communities it served. Opened on January 19, 1952, it was a toll road that quickly paid its way. The toll station was located at the Broomfield turnoff; the last day tolls were collected was September 14, 1967. *Courtesy* Daily Camera, *Boulder*.

V

A FUTURE NOT BY DEFAULT,
BUT BY DESIGN
1970–1991

A CLASH OF THE OLD AND THE NEW inaugurated the seventies and gave a glimpse of the future. In one corner sat the old champion of "grow or die"; in the other, the upstart environmental challenger, "quality of life." The scrap started innocently enough over what seemed at first to be a real feather in the cap of Colorado: a successful bid to host the 1976 Winter Olympics.

Costs to be borne by the host, both financial and environmental, led to the conflict. The pro-Olympic forces, which included Governor John Love, Denver Mayor William McNichols, Denver organizers, and much of Colorado's business community, were caught off guard by the vocal grass roots opposition. The foes, Citizens for Colorado's Future, raised issues of potential cost overruns, environmental impacts, questionable profits, and misleading claims by the organizers. They scorned the "Sell Colorado" approach and rejected the smog, traffic problems, unneeded growth, and debt that the Games would bring. A ballot issue that prohibited state funds from being used to underwrite expenses was voted on in the 1972 election. It attracted the publicity that some promoters had wanted for Colorado, but the results were not what had been expected. Sixty percent of the voters approved the measure, and the Olympics were forced to move elsewhere.

The vote was really one for conservation and environment; taxpayers wanted their money to go for something other than stimulating growth. The pro-Olympics faction had blundered badly and misjudged the changing attitudes of Coloradans. For the first time in the history of the state, the idea of "Sell Colorado" had been dealt a major blow. Environmental awareness was clearly long overdue, as evidenced by Denver's "brown cloud," statewide traffic and highway problems, urban and rural sprawl, mounting tons of trash, water pollution, and lack of planning.

The Winter Olympics controversy focused attention on protecting Colorado's future as nothing else had done for a generation. Coloradans had voiced their opinions, much to the chagrin of the old guard. The vote also helped place Richard Lamm, one of the leading opponents of bringing the Olympics to Colorado, in the governor's chair for three terms. He, more than any other Colorado governor in history, focused attention on those issues that had to be discussed and dealt with—environment, overpopulation, the graying of America, soaring medical costs, and immigration. Many citizens were shocked at his bluntness when discussing these subjects, which were not necessarily new but until now had been largely ignored. With some provocative statements, Governor Lamm forced an examination of these questions. Despite having more than his share of troubles with the conservative Republican-controlled legislature, Lamm left a legacy of raised consciences to his state.

Democrats, who had had little success in taking control of the legislature, held tightly to the governorship as Roy Romer succeeded Lamm in 1987. Romer, who subsequently won reelection, pushed hard to make worldwide contacts for Colorado businesses and to increase investment in all parts of the state. His was a "Sell Colorado" administration, but an environmentally aware one. During this period, maverick Colorado voters elected both liberal and conservative U.S. senators. William Armstrong and Gary Hart were worlds apart politically, as were some of the congressional representatives, such as Ken Kramer and Pat Schroeder. It never paid to try to label Coloradans — they voted for the candidates and the issues. Political party labels held less and less attraction. The reins of political power, more than ever before, were in the hands of the Front Range cities and counties; the eastern and western portions of the state marched along as mere spear-carriers.

What did the composite Coloradan look like? The census of 1970 gave a picture of "Mr. and Mrs. Average Coloradan." They had been born outside the state, but their two children were native-born. They lived in a city (or suburb) and were young, median age 28.2 years (younger than the national median age of 30), with a family income of $9,555 per year. They were high school graduates with some college work (again better than the national average), owned their home and one car, and were on the verge of buying a second vehicle. Most had moved once in the past five years to a new home in the same county. They lived in a state that was growing much faster than the national average and, as a result, had earned another seat in the House of Representatives. Younger and better educated, they had values different from earlier generations, a trait shown no more clearly than by the Olympics vote.

Colorado residents of the seventies had plenty of other pressing problems on which to focus their attention and action. None seemed more immediately urgent than the one involving oil shale. Colorado was known to harbor some of the nation's largest reserves and had already cycled through several minor shale booms and busts. In the early 1970s the volatile political situation in the Middle East jeopardized, then temporarily closed (via the Arab oil embargo), America's chief oil sources, raising pump prices and threatening to cause long-term shortages. The cry went out for the country to become oil-independent. Oil shale, which produced mineral oil through the process of retorting, would be a major player in this scenario.

As early as 1971 the forecast promised that oil shale would produce unprecedented growth for Garfield, Mesa, and Rio Blanco counties. Projections pictured half a million people living there by the end of the century. It was estimated that Colorado had enough oil shale reserves to last 400 years; surely the crisis had been resolved. Plans went forward to exploit the deposits and develop an economical retorting method. The ramifications took on new meaning when the world's largest company, Exxon, entered the scene in mid-1980 with plans to spend $5 billion on its Colony oil shale project. The quiet Colorado River Valley and surrounding counties braced for an invasion.

By that time Coloradans were well aware of the environmental and development costs that could accompany the Exxon project. Governor Lamm warned that the state was not eager to repeat the disastrous boom-and-bust cycles it had experienced in the past. Air and water pollution (an estimated 700 billion barrels of soot!), loss of game habitat, money for such public services as roads and schools, and all the other problems of booming growth had been anticipated and discussed. Plans had been formulated to meet those challenges. Grand Junction boomed as it had not since the uranium rush. Parachute and other small towns experienced unprecedented growth, and an entirely new community, Battlement Mesa, left the drawing boards and moved into construction.

The *Denver Post* followed Lamm's warning with one of its own: "A surging shale industry doesn't have to do simply with oil. A surging shale industry involves roads and schools, law enforcement and medical services, domestic water supply and pollution control — a myriad of human concerns, all of which are Colorado's concerns" (June 29, 1980). Coloradans and many others ignored the warnings. The potential economic benefits blinded oil-boomers to the lessons of history.

Then, on Sunday, May 2, 1982, it all went bust. Exxon abruptly announced the closing of its Colony project. The declining price of oil on the world market, and the fact that an economical retorting method had not been found, ended the company's interest in shale, even though billions of dollars had already been spent. The region would be affected for the rest of the decade. Grand Junction's real estate market collapsed, and residents throughout the region endured foreclosures, bankruptcies, and divorces caused by "emotional and financial stress." More than that was involved, however, as historian Andrew Gulliford pointed out in his *Boomtown Blues:* "In retrospect, Black Sunday on the Western Slope was the falling domino that sent the 'oil patch' states of Oklahoma, Texas and Louisiana into an economic tailspin." The economic distress of those states would haunt Colorado for a long time.

The cycle was repeated on a smaller scale in towns such as Hayden, Oak Creek, and Craig, which were near the strip-mineable coal deposits. The same energy crisis that created the oil shale monster also raised the possibility of substituting coal for oil. In the seventies a coal surge came, bringing with it giant power plants. It transformed the region before local and state governments were ready. The results were predictable. By 1978 real estate prices had skyrocketed in Craig, trailer houses were becoming eyesores, the water system lay in shambles, schools were overcrowded, and the population had doubled. When the boom eventually subsided, the local economy took a slide.

Denver, in the meantime, profited when many of the energy companies relocated there during the boom, a circumstance the city quickly took advantage of by proclaiming itself the "energy capital of the United States." A *New York Times* reporter visited the city in March 1974 and did not like what he saw. The newcomers moving in at the rate of 1,200 a week were "creating a big city with big problems." Denver's air was polluted, its crime on the rise. Traffic jams had become common and the community was surrounded by sprawling suburbs "filled with enough neon, plastic and ticky-tacky to fill a baby Los Angeles." New arrivals crowded into the mountains west of the city. Needless to say, these pessimistic observations were not well received in Denver.

Somewhere between the experiences of Craig and Grand Junction on the one hand and Denver on the other, a frightening look at the future could be had. Colorado's quality of life and its environment appeared to be held hostage by Washington's strategy of satisfying pressing fuel and energy demands. To their credit, Coloradans stood up to the challenge and kept environmental issues and quality of life in the forefront of their thinking.

Most of rural Colorado fell outside the boom, creating problems of another kind. A 1975–76 study showed, for instance, that the beloved rural physician was becoming extinct. Counties on the plains, and some in the mountains, were finding it extremely difficult to attract and keep doctors. Nine of the sixty-three counties had no physicians at all, and fifteen others had three or fewer. (In contrast, Denver, Arapahoe, Jefferson, and Boulder counties had over 80 percent of the state's doctors.) Many of these same counties lost population and businesses during this time, which diluted their political power and dimmed their futures. The mountain counties did not suffer the same afflictions as their plains neighbors. Breckenridge lamented its too-rapid growth, which brought shoddy construction, greedy promoters, and out-of-state hucksters to its attractive ski slopes. Breckenridge's circumstances paled in comparison to Aspen's. A 1977 feature story in *Sports Illustrated* described that former mining town as the "Land of Peter Pan." Overexploitation of skiing and tourism caused Aspen to lose much of its charm.

One age-old dream finally came to fruition — an automobile tunnel under the Continental Divide. For over a generation Loveland Pass had been examined as a potential site for it. The project was finally begun in 1968 after much planning. It took five years, and nearly $1,100 per inch, to build the Eisenhower Tunnel, which opened in 1973. It proved so popular that a second bore was driven to carry the increased traffic. Skiing and tourism were the big beneficiaries as traffic was expedited along Interstate 70 between Denver and Grand Junction.

Against this background the state celebrated its centennial. It hardly seemed that one hundred years had passed since the Centennial State was welcomed into the union. On that August 1 anniversary in 1976, the *Denver Post* took occasion to look back at the triumphs and tragedies of the past century. It expressed the hope that Coloradans had "learned a great deal" by their mistakes. For the future, the editorial called for "balanced growth," the development of water supplies, responsible land-use regulations, and effective transportation networks. The good life had been vigorously pursued for over a century. Now the ground rules had changed, and along with them the goals of Coloradans.

They had already expressed their preference for limitations on growth. Now they warned that tourism was getting out of hand. Ski slopes, parks, national forests, and mountain valleys were becoming overcrowded and disgustingly littered (a situation not solely attributable to out-of-staters). They also saw some of their heritage disappearing under the wrecker's ball. Denver deserved particular condemnation for neglect in this area until preservation-conscious residents came to the rescue with organizations and laws. Colorado had so much history to lose that preservation became a volatile issue statewide. It would be a struggle to maintain the old, but a cause worth fighting for.

In April 1981 Leon Martel, executive vice president of the Hudson Institute, addressed Colorado's prospects. He forecast that the state would continue to attract people, that national dependence on traditional energy sources would impact the region, and that the future would be different. He warned that Colorado should make sure it was not "stuck with the costs of growth," which should be paid by developers and users. Most important, Martel gave some advice that all Coloradans should heed: "Plan long-term so that successors 100 years or more from now find a future not by default, but by design."

Noted Denver editorial writer Bill Hornby came back to the same subject in a 1989 article. Growth, he wrote, will happen "whether you or I like it or not . . . So why not be an optimist about 'growth'? Why not plan for it and build for it, so that the greater numbers who will be living here by the year 2000 can live in decent harmony, rather than indecent hassle?"

As the eighties moved on, default and indecent hassle too often triumphed over design and harmony. Coloradans bickered among themselves. Western Slope residents took on the Eastern Slope over water, among other things. Plains residents complained that they were being ignored and abandoned by the rest of the state. Denver and Aurora (which had the third-highest national growth rate among cities) sometimes seemed to relish their rivalry, but underneath it lay an acrimonious struggle to dominate. Like other Americans, Coloradans sued each other in record numbers. Testiness and uncertainty characterized the times.

In one respect, though, times never changed — nature continued to follow its fancy. The Big Thompson flood of July 1976, which killed 151 people, and the tornado that devastated Limon fourteen years later were only two major examples of the weather's vagaries. Droughts hurt farmers and ski operators alike, hail leveled wheat fields on the eastern plains, snowstorms hampered transportation everywhere (and caused some classic traffic jams in Denver), and late frosts ruined fruit crops on the Western Slope. Over the years Coloradans suffered millions of dollars' worth of damage at nature's hand on the plains and in the mountains.

The search for new sources of revenue to meet ever-increasing demands created other kinds of problems. One novel experiment of the 1980s was the introduction of the state lottery, a supposedly painless way to raise funds. Harkening back to something that had been tried in the nineteenth century in many states, it allowed Coloradans to have their cake and eat it, too. The plan proposed to use most of the money raised by the lottery for parks and recreation, but the legislature found the lack of prisons more pressing (crime was a growing problem in both urban and rural areas), and the majority of the funds were eventually funneled in that direction. New prisons, however, did not alleviate crime or rehabilitate prisoners. Meanwhile, interest in buying lottery tickets lagged, so lotto was added, with two drawings per week for much larger prizes. The economic windfall from these measures did not prove to be what the originators had predicted, but the games lived on.

Mining and agriculture, once the bedrock of the economy, fizzled, casualties of national and international influences more than any specific Colorado crisis. No easy solution reversed the agricultural woes or the rural decline. The causes were old — low prices, surpluses, debt, and foreign competition. When farmers abandoned their land, the nearby communities suffered, too. A Yuma County farmer summed up the situation very well: "I'll take responsibility for expanding too fast in the 1970s, but the banks were too willing to extend the credit, and farmers were too willing to take it." To make matters worse, the federal government cut back on its subsidies and assistance, pushing agriculture closer to the brink of disaster. Critics of government programs advocated their elimination; defenders believed that without them farmers would go broke. There was no ready answer. Meanwhile, the taxpayer was picking up a sizeable share of the tab for the annual harvest.

Water created another source of conflict for the farmer: was the best use of this vital commodity rural or urban? Most of the dollars beckoned from the cities. Aurora, for instance, purchased water rights in the Rocky Ford area, eliciting fears there for the future of local agriculture. Said one disgruntled farmer, "The root of the whole thing is the God-almighty dollar. All these educated [beeps] want to make a dollar off somebody else's sweat." Nevertheless, conditions had changed, and the best use for that water was a legitimate question. The fight was destined to be a long, emotional one. Even nontributary groundwater (aquifers — nonrenewable subsurface reservoirs) was under consideration for claim-filing until the Colorado Supreme Court held in 1983 that it was not subject to appropriation. Over 100 lawyers represented various concerned parties at the hearing, graphically demonstrating the interest in water. On the debate's outcome would hinge the future of rural Colorado.

Water projects were not so easy to come by as they once had been. The Animas/La Plata, in the southwestern corner of the state, had been in the planning stage for a generation and still had not seen the light of day. Politically active opponents, endangered-species laws, and rising costs seriously threatened its future. Denver and its suburbs received a similar setback when the federal government ended plans to build Two Forks Dam on the South Platte River. Environmental effects and serious concerns about cost and need sank the project, although a few unreconstructed supporters continued a lonely fight to resurrect it.

In contrast to the eastern plains were high-riding Aspen and Pitkin County, among the most expensive places in the country to buy a home. Coloradans were fascinated to learn in the early 1980s that the median value of a house there topped $200,000. Skiing costs were also escalating rapidly. At the end of the decade, the $50-a-day lift ticket seemed imminent. Out-of-state competition for skiers increased as the number of them leveled off during the decade, bringing some trepidation to the ski industry. Americans were getting older, and the youthful image attached to skiing needed to be revamped to tap a growing market. The Colorado ski industry looked for revitalization in the 1990s. Skier visits (one person skiing one day) did go up slightly during the 1990–91 season to nearly 9.8 million, still below the record ten million.

The mining industry, regrettably, did not warrant much optimism. The oil and oil shale crashes devastated the industry and its Denver headquarters. Companies folded or retrenched while idleness overtook the fields and the geologists. Mining engineers and other workers took to the streets in search of work. Competition from open-pit mines in Nevada, a lower international price, and restrictive environmental laws pushed gold and silver mining to the edge of extinction. The *Rocky Mountain News* told the story: "Colorado, although headquarters to the U.S. gold mining industry, has seen its own gold production fall 41 percent since 1978" (March 12, 1991). Coal strip-mining managed to hang on while underground coal mining declined. Out of mining's recession would emerge leaner, more modernized, more technologically advanced companies — as the *Denver Post* called them, a "new breed of operators" (September 24, 1989). Before mining could again play a large role in Colorado, though, it had to face up to the environmental issues it raised.

All of these factors produced a trend that disintegrated into a mid-decade slump. Colorado's postwar growth and economic boom came to an end. In a January 26, 1986, article, a *Denver Post* reporter graphically described what was happening. The construction and housing industries had slowed, the number of jobs had declined and unemployment had increased, the per capita income had slipped (Colorado dropped from sixth to fortieth nationally), the number of people moving into the state had fallen off, and the state was losing its most highly educated residents to more attractive positions elsewhere. (Before the slump hit, Colorado had six of the top twenty-five counties in the country in terms of the highest number of college-educated residents.) The article could have said also that the growth rate had slowed, that economic slumps in Wyoming and Montana had hurt Colorado, that local and state governments were postponing capital-intensive projects (one jarring indicator — roads got steadily worse), that tourism had flattened and the average tourist was spending less, and that revenue for all levels of government was sharply limited. Reflecting on the plight of the tourist business, a Crested Butte resident pointedly observed, "We can no longer take it for granted that people will just pour in here. We have a big challenge ahead of us." All of these things together spelled recession. Colorado was not an isolated example, but for its residents, who had not experienced something so severe in over a generation, it came as a shock.

Symbolic of the depth of the crisis was the failure of Silverado Banking, Savings and Loan, one of Denver's high-flying financial institutions. Both the bank and Denver lived well until 1985, when oil prices broke, construction sagged, and bankruptcies escalated. Silverado was only one part of the disastrous nationwide failure of savings and loan institutions, but it was Colorado's biggest collapse and one of the worst in the country. Silverado (seized by federal regulators in December 1988) was wrecked by poor management, soured real estate deals, enrichment of top officials, "creative" bookkeeping, and questionable lending practices. An article in *US News and World Report* (August 13, 1990) characterized Silverado as a "rich model to understanding the forces that brought down hundreds of similar thrifts across the country." Regulators failed to take preventive action, despite plenty of warning, until far too late, and taxpayers were left holding the bill to bail out the defunct savings and loans. Another prosperous era died in the ashes of this sad story. The "swaggering cockiness" of Silverado's key officials cost the state and its residents much more than the bank had ever generated in business and publicity.

Like Silverado, but in a different realm, the Denver Broncos managed to dash the hopes of Coloradans. After years of frustrating losses, the team finally won its conference championship and went to the Super Bowl in 1978. Rarely in its history had this geographically diverse state been so united behind anything. Then the "Orange Crush" was itself crushed by Dallas, 27–10. But that loss paled in comparison to the three Super Bowl defeats that came in the 1980s, which set standards for frustration and futility. Many Denverites and Coloradans had projected their own images into that of their sports teams, and their egos suffered when their favorite team disappointed them. The state's other team, the Denver Nuggets, failed to provide any lasting relief on the basketball floor. By the 1990–91 season they had become the worst team in the NBA. To make matters worse, professional hockey, rodeo, soccer, tennis, and volleyball franchises failed to stick, as did another professional football team, the Denver Gold.

Only Denver's minor league baseball team survived, but its owners and fans preferred a major league team. Starting in 1984 a serious attempt was made to attract an existing team or secure an expansion club, but the campaign did not produce results until 1991. Denver saw itself as a major professional sports city and continued its efforts toward attaining that goal.

Big-time college athletics were now a significant part of the sports scene. The Air Force Academy, Colorado State University, and the University of Colorado all furnished moments of football and basketball glory. In 1990 CU sports fans realized their ultimate fantasy when the football team won the Big Eight Conference title, the Orange Bowl, and the national championship. The ski team also brought home a national championship.

Unfortunately, the well-established Colorado higher education system (from junior and community colleges to graduate schools) did not shine as brilliantly in academics as in sports (although a CU professor did win a Nobel prize). Colorado's overextended system found itself beset with a multitude of difficulties as the 1990s opened. Some colleges watched enrollments drop; others experienced a desperate need for new buildings. All endured financial stresses. The state legislature discovered that the educational bill for public and higher education was eating up more than half of the annual budget. Education had become big business — and that business came at a cost. The future would not wait for financing — Coloradans and their legislators would have to come to grips with the problem now.

The Coloradans who faced the dilemmas of 1990 were collectively older than those of twenty years earlier, their median age being 32, and they had fewer children. They also enjoyed a higher per capita income of $18,404. They were more optimistic than they had been for a while — a poll showed that they expected an economic upswing in the coming decade. Environmental matters continued to hold their attention, as did the aging of America, which would "likely threaten the tourist industry, which does not cater to older people." The end of the cold war brought relief but also proved to be a mixed blessing for Colorado's economy, which for the past two generations had been closely tied to the military-industrial complex through government contracts and military bases. Colorado Springs and Denver stood to lose in a big way if bases were closed or expenditures cut back.

Pueblo was one of the success stories that the state could point to with pride. After losing its economic linchpin, Colorado Fuel, Iron and Steel, it set out to attract new industries. It added fourteen and created over 2,000 jobs in the eighties. The Western Slope, in contrast, stayed mired in an economic slump, with mining down, agriculture hurting, and tourism only slowly improving. The downfall of the Colorado Ute Electric Association (it overbuilt for expansion that never came and suffered from poor management) was a severe blow to the area and to the eastern counties it also served. In some ways this statewide mixed economic bag revived memories of a century before, when the early 1890s looked both promising and precarious. Colorado had traveled this road before, but many Coloradans lacked the historical perspective to learn from those earlier lessons. They were fated to have to master again what history could have taught them. One of CU's presidents, George Norlin, expressed it well: "Who knows only his own generation remains always a child."

Colorado 1991 provided glimpses of both past and future. The rural-versus-urban fight continued along with the water issues. The Silverado fiasco finally drew near the light at the end of the tunnel. Major league baseball knocked on Denver's door, and gambling returned to the state.

The resolution of the Silverado Banking, Savings and Loan failure slowly drew to a close as the federal government, after two years of examining 15 million documents, announced the settlement of the $200 million gross negligence lawsuit it filed against thirteen defendants; the amount agreed upon was $29.5 million. Lessons had been learned from this mess that would, it was hoped, benefit the state in the future. Inevitably, though, banking would be forever changed. Public confidence had been shaken. Just around the corner lay branch banking. With it would come innovations that would affect all Coloradans.

On a more upbeat note the Bolder Boulder, which had evolved into one of the country's premier foot races, attracted more than 30,000 runners on a beautiful May 27 morning. Running, skiing, hiking, mountain-bike riding, rafting, gardening — Coloradans embraced them all in their enthusiasm for outdoor and physical fitness activities.

Those citizens more apt to watch sports than participate in them applauded the long-awaited final confirmation that Denver had been awarded a National League baseball franchise on July 5, 1991. Opening Day would not come until 1993 for the Colorado Rockies; they would play in Mile High Stadium until construction of a new park was completed in the Platte River Valley of lower downtown. Meanwhile, Denver Bronco fans waited for the team to win another trip to the Super Bowl and achieve better results than the devastating defeats in the 1980s.

Construction on Denver's new airport began as the state tried to keep pace with increases in passenger volume and continued to wrestle with the isolation and distance problems that had plagued Colorado since 1858. The effort to persuade United Airlines to build its maintenance center in the capital city duplicated generations-old attempts to lure investment to the Rockies. There was nothing new about the state and the city offering inducements to bring in new business, but the dollar amounts and the length of time to be covered were unprecedented. This revived the conflict between rural and urban Colorado. Rural spokespeople objected to spending millions of state dollars when, as they saw it, the United deal would benefit only Denver. Their objections prompted *Denver Post* writer Mark Obmascik to remind them of the water projects and other programs that had benefited them: "But a closer look shows they also have cultivated another bumper crop — and it's called pure hypocrisy. Many Colorado farmers have been sucking so hard and so long of fat federal subsidies that their faces should be permanently puckered."

New, and yet old, was the voters' approval in November 1990 of a measure to allow three mountain mining communities — Black Hawk, Central City, and Cripple Creek — to engage in limited-stakes gambling. This return to the trappings of an earlier era was heartily approved by locals, who envisioned a financial shot in the arm for their economies. Real estate values immediately skyrocketed, and future casino owners dreamed of fortunes while refurbishing their buildings and buying needed equipment and decorations at prices that soared well into the millions of dollars. The verdict was still out on whether their efforts would be successful. Other depressed Colorado communities could only hope to somehow grab a piece of the action.

One of the lures of the gambling bill had been its promise to contribute some of the revenue to historic preservation. However, given the spotty record of the lottery in sticking to its original intent of funding parks and recreation, that promise appeared somewhat dubious. Durango, however, became the twentieth community in Colorado to establish a historic preservation ordinance and a supervisory board. Those Colorado tourist towns that marketed their Victorian heritage to visitors had much to gain by saving their architecture and historic structures.

Denver found itself mired in debt, including the $2.3 billion for the new international airport. Since 1983 the city's public debt had ballooned from virtually zero to almost $2.8 billion — a tax burden of $1,600 for every man, woman, and child. Besides the airport, funds had been spent to improve the Civic Center, build a new convention center, and completely remodel the stock show arena. These projects, designed to make the city more attractive for investors, residents, and visitors alike, also helped "to create construction jobs and spur economic growth," according to the *Denver Post* (May 26, 1991). It was a calculated risk that only the future could prove right or wrong. A representative of Moody's Investors Service, the New York bond-rating agency, placed the city's position in perspective: "Cities are always going to need to maintain themselves and provide for growth. It's give and take, a balancing act."

A new airport, a baseball team, and a reviving economy did not generate the only Denver news of 1991. Like other American cities, Denver dealt with the problems of homelessness, poverty, crime, and gang violence. It also held a historic election: for the first time in the history of a major American city, two black candidates faced off in a run-off election for mayor. The contest determined who would replace the popular Federico Peña (Denver's first Hispanic mayor), who had caught Robert Speer's vision of the "city beautiful" and updated it. The winner, Wellington Webb, came from far back in the polls to overtake Norm Early. To him would fall the major task of carrying the airport through to completion and maintaining Denver's role as the primary distribution and financial center of the Rocky Mountain states.

As had been typical for so long, Denver tended to grab headlines away from the rest of the state. Outside the capital city, however, such issues as water, national and world business environment, and historic preservation were expected to play vital roles in the future. Inflation escalated the cost of the Dolores Project to $522.8 million, an 861 percent cost overrun since its original 1970 price estimate. The neighboring Animas/La Plata Project, not yet off the ground, had increased its cost 418 percent; opponents called it the "most shameless example" of rural bailouts. Objections from various groups, including the Navajos and the state of Utah, continued to delay ground-breaking. With no more projects on the drawing boards, these appeared likely to be the last two to come out of almost ninety years of federal dam, canal, and irrigation projects in the state.

One of Denver's oldest businesses, the Gates Corporation, pointed the way to the future as it aggressively expanded its trade throughout the nation and the world. The same could be said for Coors, which had grown well beyond its Golden beginnings to become one of the country's major beer producers; in fact, Colorado brewed more beer than any other state in 1990. Silverton, however, bemoaned the closing of its last major mine, a victim of low mineral prices and declining ore values. Mounting environmental restrictions and competition from cheaper open-pit mining made it doubtful that the Sunnyside Mine would ever reopen.

Coloradans looking toward the year 2000 and a new millennium see a challenging, if somewhat uncertain, future. If they have the optimism and faith of their ancestors, they will muddle through, as each generation has. As scholar and lawyer Charles Wilkinson points out, "These are the times in which our whole generation must take a stand and define a sustainable future. If we do not, our distinctive and special places may simply pass on and be replaced by the grey and the generic."

Colorado, tamed and untamed, has faced the camera lens for over a century and a third. It has not always produced a pretty photograph, but through changing times a people's heritage has been preserved. Coloradans have, in the 1861 words of William Byers, "[secured] the shadow, ere the substance perish."

Thomas Hornsby Ferril's poem "Judging from the Tracks" captures the tenor of Colorado history:

> Man and his watchful spirit lately walked
> This misty road . . . at least the man is sure,
> Because he made his tracks so visible,
> As if he must have felt they would endure.
>
> There was no lovely demon at his side,
> A demon's tracks are beautiful and old,
> Nor is it plausible a genius walked
> Beside him here, because the prints are cold.
>
> And judging from the tracks, it's doubtful if
> A guardian angel moved above his head,
> For even thru the mist it can be seen
> That he was leading and not being led.

Vietnam War protest, May 7, 1970. *Photo by Mel Schieltz. Courtesy Denver Public Library/Western History Department.*

Building the Eisenhower Tunnel on Interstate 70, November 5, 1971. Construction cost was over $1,000 an inch. *Photo by Robert W. Schott. Courtesy Colorado Historical Society, Denver.*

University of Colorado graduate Greg Martin at commencement ceremonies, 1974. President Frederick Thieme (on left) is amused. *Courtesy Carnegie Library, Boulder.*

Farmers went on strike in eastern Colorado in 1977. Widespread foreclosures and the collapse of farm prices caused a new agrarian protest in the late 1970s. Tractor convoys and disruption of foreclosure sales focused attention on farmers' problems. *Courtesy Pueblo Library District.*

This 1977 photo graphically illustrates a point: a truckload of manure is identified as agricultural profit. *Courtesy Pueblo Library District.*

Governor Richard Lamm signs as witness to a wheat contract between Colorado growers and the Republic of China, June 15, 1978. In the last several decades, state officials have become increasingly active in promoting Colorado products abroad. *Courtesy Colorado Historical Society, Denver.*

Former president Gerald Ford and Eddie Box at Durango centennial, 1980. Ford, part owner of KIUP radio station, participated in several events. *Courtesy Fort Lewis College/Center of Southwest Studies, Durango.*

Rodolpho "Corky" Gonzales, August 14, 1980. Gonzalez emerged as an important figure in Denver in the 1960s as director of the Neighborhood Youth Corps and chair of the War on Poverty program. In 1966 he launched the Crusade for Justice and later helped found Colorado's La Raza Unida. *Photo by Dave Buresh. Courtesy Colorado Historical Society, Denver.*

The "jungle buster" is used to push over dead trees and smash everything left after logging. This work was once done by hand to help a new forest to grow. Church's Park area in Middle Park, 1980. *Courtesy Grand County Museum, Hot Sulphur Springs.*

Colowyo coal mine in Axial Basin south of Craig, 1981. Coal mining is of major importance in this area. *Courtesy Museum of Northwest Colorado, Craig.*

PROTOTYPE TRACT C-b
OCT. 31 1980
AREA OIL SHALE OFFICE

Oil shale development, Rio Blanco County, 1980. The Piceance Basin has been the center of considerable oil shale activity. *Photo by R. L. Elderkin, Jr. Courtesy U.S. Geological Survey, Denver.*

The Colony oil shale project near Parachute, 1981. Exxon bought into Colony in 1980 and began aggressive development, only to cancel the project suddenly in May 1982; 2,100 people were thrown out of work overnight. It was another case of the boom-and-bust syndrome that has characterized the extractive industries throughout Colorado's history. *Photo by R. L. Elderkin, Jr. Courtesy U.S. Geological Survey, Denver.*

Like a ghost from an earlier age, the Coney Island hot dog stand sits near Highway 285 west of Denver. This long-popular road takes the traveler up Turkey Creek Canyon to Bailey and over Kenosha Pass into South Park. *Photo by Glenn Cuerden. Courtesy Glenn Cuerden, Denver.*

A homeless man in Denver in the 1980s. *Photo by Glenn Cuerden. Courtesy Glenn Cuerden, Denver.*

Protestors encircle the controversial nuclear weapons plant at Rocky Flats in the early 1980s. *Courtesy University of Colorado/Western Historical Collections, Boulder.*

Gay rights march, downtown Denver. Social ferment continued in Colorado and the rest of the nation in the 1980s and 1990s. *Photo by Glenn Cuerden. Courtesy Glen Cuerden, Denver.*

Part of the Frying Pan–Arkansas Project at Twin Lakes. This massive project diverts water from the Frying Pan into tunnels through the Continental Divide for the benefit of Front Range communities, thereby causing resentment on the Western Slope. New plans for similar diversions continue to generate heated debate. *Courtesy Bureau of Reclamation, Denver.*

Penstocks on Bald Mountain and the Flatiron power and pumping plant are in the delivery system of the Northern Colorado Water Conservancy District. The scope of the district demonstrates the significance of water in Colorado; it includes Dillon and Green Mountain reservoirs to the west and diverts water through the Continental Divide. *Courtesy Northern Colorado Water Conservancy District, Loveland.*

Author Louis L'Amour drew a crowd wherever he appeared in Colorado. Many of his novels had Colorado settings, and he wrote several while visiting the state. He owned a ranch east of Mancos. *Courtesy the* Durango Herald.

Hikers on the Beaverbrook Trail on Lookout Mountain in Jefferson County, 1986. Robert Speer's dream of a Denver Mountain Park system became a reality and is now widely enjoyed. *Photo by Tom Noel. Courtesy Tom Noel, Denver.*

Ben Nighthorse Campbell campaigns for the U.S. House of Representatives in 1986. Campbell, who won the 3rd District seat, is part Cheyenne, the only American Indian in Congress. *Courtesy Ben Nighthorse Campbell, Ignacio.*

The Denver Broncos gave Coloradans something to cheer about — and something to shed tears about. The team won four American Football Conference championships in the 1970s and 1980s but lost in the Super Bowl all four times. This 1989 game against the New York Giants was a rematch of Super Bowl XXI. *Courtesy the* Durango Herald.

The Denver & Rio Grande Western ski train, 1989. Skiers use the Interstate highways to reach some ski areas, but the train to Winter Park remains a sellout on weekends. *Photo by Tom Noel. Courtesy Tom Noel, Denver.*

Saturdays on East Colfax in Denver — the seamier side of urban life, 1989. *Courtesy Tom Noel, Denver.*

Rebuilding the Durango & Silverton Railroad roundhouse in Durango after the 1989 fire. Concerned railroad buffs from throughout the world wrote the company to inquire about the fate of the roundhouse. *Courtesy Durango & Silverton Railroad, Durango.*

The uranium mining boom of the 1950s and 1960s brought then-unrecognized health hazards. Low levels of radiation in the Vanadium Corporation's tailings pile on the edge of Durango prompted the Environmental Protection Agency to remove the tailings to a covered site in 1989. *Courtesy M. K. Ferguson Company, Albuquerque.*

Little Dry Creek Plaza, an urban renewal project in Englewood, ca. 1990. *Courtesy Englewood Public Library.*

The Denver Public Library asked voters to approve a 1990 bond issue to raise money for the remodeling of the building. The measure passed, clearing the way for an expansion of the library. *Photo by Roger Whitacre. Courtesy Tom Noel, Denver.*

Three generations of the Charlie Lemon family and friends move cows from their summer range in La Plata County, autumn 1990. *Photo by Richard Ellis. Courtesy Fort Lewis College/Center of Southwest Studies, Durango.*

Climax was once Colorado's largest and richest mining operation, but it suspended production in the mid-eighties because of a declining market and worldwide competition. Leadville suffered as the miners left, but in mid-1991 a small-scale reopening was planned. The company town is gone, but the mine plant remains on the crest of Fremont Pass. *Photo by Richard Ellis. Courtesy Fort Lewis College/Center of Southwest Studies, Durango.*

Uranium mine, 1990. By the late 1980s only a few small operations remained. The boom-and-bust cycle had run its course, leaving behind a legacy of broken dreams and "hot" mine dumps. The plateau country of the state's western border returned to the peace and quiet of earlier days. *Photo by Richard Ellis. Courtesy Fort Lewis College/Center of Southwest Studies, Durango.*

About 1,000 people turned out in Durango to greet members of the 928th Medical Company upon its return from the Persian Gulf on May 10, 1991. *Photo by Miles Davies. Courtesy* Durango Herald.

Railroads continue to be important for the Colorado economy. A Denver & Rio Grande Western freight train heads up the Arkansas Valley south of Leadville in June 1991. *Photo by Richard Ellis. Courtesy Fort Lewis College/Center of Southwest Studies, Durango.*

Skier Matt Bryniarski with volunteer Mike Hiltman run the course at the annual Football Players Ski Race for the disabled. This race is part of the program of the Durango/Purgatory Handicapped Sports Association founded in 1983. *Photo by Scott Warren. Courtesy Beth Warren, Durango/Purgatory Handicapped Sports Association.*

"Ride the Rockies" bike tour on Highway 160 east of Durango, June 1991. More than 2,000 participated in the ride from Cortez to Denver. *Photo by Richard Ellis. Courtesy Fort Lewis College/Center of Southwest Studies, Durango.*

Commercial rafting on the Arkansas River below Texas Creek, June 1991. Rafting has developed into a major seasonal commercial operation on many Colorado rivers and has caused some conflict with other sports enthusiasts. *Photo by Richard Ellis. Courtesy Fort Lewis College/Center of Southwest Studies, Durango.*

Kayaker doing an "ender" in the Animas River, June 1991. River sports gained tremendous popularity in the eighties and early nineties. *Courtesy the* Durango Herald.

Tourists board the early morning run of the Durango & Silverton Railroad, June 1991. Once the major connection between Silverton's mines and Durango's smelters, the line has operated solely for tourists since the 1960s. *Photo by Richard Ellis. Courtesy Fort Lewis College/Center of Southwest Studies, Durango.*

The popularity of living in the mountains has placed great pressure on Colorado's natural environment. Developments are found from the foothills west, such as Fairfield Pagosa. *Photo by Richard Ellis. Courtesy Fort Lewis College/Center of Southwest Studies, Durango.*

Tourists come to enjoy the great out-of-doors and then crowd together in campgrounds and trailer parks. Fun Valley on the eastern approach to Wolf Creek Pass is one of the popular spots. *Photo by Richard Ellis. Courtesy Fort Lewis College/Center of Southwest Studies, Durango.*

Sprinkler irrigation near San Acacio in the San Luis Valley, June 1991. Agriculture is still of great significance in the valley. *Photo by Richard Ellis. Courtesy Fort Lewis College/Center of Southwest Studies, Durango.*

The old west and the new west merge in Colorado as the twentieth century draws to a close. This sheepherders camp is located north of Hayden. 1991. *Photo by Richard Ellis. Courtesy Fort Lewis College/Center of Southwest Studies, Durango.*

Peter Coors greets participants in the Coors Environmental Wellness Fair at the brewery in Golden, June 11, 1991. *Courtesy Coors Brewing Company, Golden.*

Coloradans and others race for fun, a sense of accomplishment, and for the enjoyment of being involved in this world-famous race. Colorado as a state was racing into an unclear future at the same time. Nineteen ninety-one was half gone, and a new millennium was only a few years away. *Photo by Cliff Grassmick. Courtesy* Daily Camera, *Boulder*.

INDEX